HAWTHORN FARM

FRED ARCHER

Illustrations by Michael Barnard

SUTTON PUBLISHING

First published in 1998 by
Sutton Publishing Limited · Phoenix Mill
Thrupp · Stroud · Gloucestershire · GL5 2BU

British Library Cataloguing in Publication Data
A catalogue record for this book is available from the British Library

ISBN 0 7509 1422 6

™ ALAN SUTTON™ and SUTTON™ are the
trade marks of Sutton Publishing Limited

Typeset in 12/15 pt Garamond.
Typesetting and origination by
Sutton Publishing Limited.
Printed in Great Britain by
MPG Books Ltd, Bodmin, Cornwall.

CONTENTS

PREFACE

This book is a word-picture of life on the farm and in the rural village from 1940 until 1980, a period during which the Agricultural Revolution has accelerated to a pace that could be described as somewhat frightening. It is the story of one particular farm – Hawthorn Farm in Worcestershire – but it could be any farm, in any village, as it weaves its way through four decades.

The farm has changed out of all recognition over the last seventy years, from the corduroyed, hobnail-booted clodhoppers who cut a narrow swathe with the three-horse binder, to the smart operative in white overalls with his twenty-foot wide combine harvester, car, and holidays abroad. A far cry from the carter and cowman of those days – not really so distant – when a second-hand bicycle was a luxury, and the only holidays were Good Friday, Easter Day and Christmas Day.

This tale begins in the late 1930s, when Hawthorn Farm and its fruit trees lay abandoned and semi-derelict. Thomas Dudley, who took over the farm, was a Midlands industrialist. His story is the first to be told. He farmed in a traditional style except that his workforce consisted mainly of Italian prisoners of war and land girls. What a shock those land girls gave to the status quo! The staid women workers who had done women's work on the land – pea picking, onion tying – were not expected to drive tractors, stook corn, load the hay, or milk cows. But the land girls proved themselves; girls whose hair reeked of tobacco from working in Wills Factory, they proved their mettle on the land.

Thomas Dudley came when prices were fixed for English apples, all one price if they were more than 2½ inches in diameter. He fed the trees, nourished and nurtured them, and reaped the harvest.

Major Sanderson followed Thomas Dudley, taking over the farm after the war. He had all the traits of a kindly gentleman farmer at

Hawthorn Farm. His war record we knew little of until his death, but we remembered him as one of the 'greats' on the village scene. He proved to be a man of the people, but unfortunately the people, his workforce, robbed him. The war robbed the farm too. Men who left the land for the forces and industry never returned. Life after this would never be the same again; the war was a watershed in more ways than one. Though the countrymen did not return, the village was replenished by an influx of townsfolk. They liked to live in the countryside, but they did not come to work on the land – the village was ideally situated for their factories and offices in Cheltenham and beyond.

The arrival of Lionel Bainbridge at Hawthorn Farm was significant. He took just a few acres, and George Burford, his old gardener, and his chauffeur Phil Grafton, were enough labour for the ground. The rest of the land was absorbed by a neighbouring farm.

Heather, Lionel's young daughter, was determined to get involved in farming. While at college she helped with lambing and calving on the farm of a girlfriend's father. Then she fell in love with Colin, a young farmer, and became a leading light in the Young Farmers Club. This caused great conflict with her father, a stockbroker, who had plans for her to marry a merchant banker. To arrange a marriage, as Lionel would have done, may seem heavy-handed today but this was a time when parents thought they had a God-given right to approve, or disapprove, of the love life of their children. A marriage was often disapproved of because of a difference in religion or in social standing. Oh, one heard of arranged marriages in India and eastern countries and this was generally frowned upon by all, but it happened here too. Maybe today, though, there is too much liberation.

Yet Lionel Bainbridge was not one of the worst type of incomer. He did have time for the Church and the local pub, where bread and cheese, an onion and cider were served as often as scampi and chips and short drinks are today. Colin had a hard time but survived as a good dairy farmer, and Heather fought for the farmer she loved.

Bernard Miles, later Lord Miles, first suggested to me that I could write a play on village and farm life. Both of us felt that something could be written chronologically about country families. Bernard, now sadly no longer with us, had given a glowing review of an earlier book of mine called *Under the Parish Lantern*. I decided on a book not a play.

Hawthorn Farm describes the folk who came to live and work there before, during and after the Second World War. The names are fictitious, but the people and their adventures are real.

I hope you like it.

CHAPTER ONE

HAWTHORN FARM

Thomas Dudley bought Hawthorn Farm at the outbreak of the Second World War in 1939. The wealthy Birmingham industrialist took over a semi-derelict 350-acre property in Worcestershire and soon transformed it into a productive holding. Hawthorn Farm was a mixture of vale and hill land. The Hill had grown little grass, being partly covered with trees known as The Roughs. The orchards in the Vale had been neglected, the unpruned trees cried out for fertilizer.

Thomas was fortunate to have connections in industry, which enabled him to get machinery and fertilizer, both severely rationed to his neighbours. Soon the hill land was cleared of thistles, and The Roughs expertly pruned by Joe Woodman. Some of this timber was sold for the production of matches, other soft woods for electricity poles – Britain, starved of foreign imports, provided a ready market for timber. Under the supervision of Mark Dale, the agricultural college trained bailiff, young trees were planted infilling the ones felled in The Roughs. After a couple of years the Vale orchard began producing fruit such as had not been seen for a lifetime. Was it the sulphate of potash which Thomas gave unstintingly to the orchards?

Harry Lock, the stockman, also ploughed and cultivated with two fine Suffolk horses. Harry and his family came to the farm and lived in a house among The Roughs. He was a good stockman with sheep and cattle but Mark Dale never trusted him – he was known to be light-fingered. One must admire young Mark, a product of Cirencester Agricultural College, for keeping a check on Lock. Old Ted Green said of him: 'What unt too hot unt too heavy for Lock. Too crooked to lie straight in bed.'

The Birmingham industrialist certainly made an impact on the village. He bought a black and white Elizabethan house, called Tudor House, in an apple orchard and with 7 acres of land adjoining the rickyard at Hawthorn Farm. On his weekend visits to the farm he became known as a stickler for tidiness, and looking at the two Suffolk horses in their shabby harness he told Mark Dale: 'Take the pair to the saddler and get them measured for new harness, both for long gears and fillers tackle. I'm not having my team with harness patched up with string.'

As petrol was rationed Tom Dudley had the idea of driving around the Hill of a Sunday afternoon in a Governess car, pulled by a cob. It was a good sight in those wartime years to see the Dudleys with their smart turn-out trotting around the lanes.

Mark Dale, the bailiff of Hawthorn Farm, became quite a friend of mine. From him I learnt some of the farming techniques practised at Cirencester. He was under Professor Boutflour, who fed milking cows with enormous amounts of protein and milked them three times a day. Mark gathered from me my experience of farming during those war years. As I had lived in the village it was easy for me to provide him with some of the local customs and, more importantly, with news about who could be trusted and who did an honest day's work.

At the local National Farmers' Union meetings we strappers in our twenties listened to the wisdom of the ancients. Some of the old farmers were doubtful of the antics of the War Agricultural Committee. At one meeting the subject of bulls on free range getting loose and serving neighbouring farmers' young heifers when they were much too young caused a lot of controversy. One old farmer summed it up this way: 'Mr Chairman, 'tis like this; if you get young heifers in a field and your neighbour's bull is the other side of the fence it's only human nature for that bull to get through the fence.'

'Human' nature, I thought! Mark smiled too and later reminded me of a mistake he made at Hawthorn Farm when he got the local vet to inject Thomas Dudley's Shorthorn herd to encourage them to come into season, or to be what is called bulling. His Shorthorn bull was so frustrated when a lot of them came on bulling the same day.

'We all make mistakes, Mark,' I said, and recalled the time when I did not take the advice of my old cowman, and as a result an oat rick got so hot it was on the point of fire. It came after a storm of rain over-night. Half the field of oat sheaves had already been carried. A field of wheat was in the next field. The cowman said: 'It's not a good thing to carry and rick the oats being so damp. Don't you think we ought to carry the wheat. Oats when damp get hot in the rick, wheat straw is hard and the sheaves don't be so close together. Wheat can be carried on the damp side.'

'Oh, we will finish the oat rick,' I said, young and inexperienced. . . . Some days later the rick began to steam.

'I told you what would happen; it's getting devilish hot.'

Days after we turned the rick onto new ground. Standing on the sheaves the heat burned our feet and the golden ears, known as flights, had turned brown. It took all day to turn the rick and prevent a fire and Old Ted Green, standing at the roadside, called out these words: 'Have you lost a watch?' This bit of sarcasm was a common expression when a hot rick had to be turned.

As neighbours, Mark and I did revolutionise one harvest-time practice, which had been common for over a hundred years. Before a field was cut with the binder, men with bagging hooks or even scythes did what was known as 'opening up', that is, they made a road around the headland of the field so that the horses and the machine didn't trample the crop. A.G. Street, writing in the *Farmers Weekly*, said this was an unnecessary practice, explaining that he drove a tractor through the corn and then, after the field had been circled several times, he went around the other way with the binder's fingers and knife as low as possible. This way less corn was wasted than when the time-honoured 'opening up' procedure was carried out.

So we tried it. Young Roy drove my tractor, and I rode the binder. The cowman thought we had gone mad, saying he had never seen such a damn stupid thing in his life – but afterwards he had to admit that hardly any corn was wasted. Mark did the same thing during his harvest and the labour-saving idea spread around.

After a couple of years in Ayshon, Mark Dale fitted in to wartime village life. He and Mary occupied the farmhouse known as The Hawthorns. He was a smart young farm bailiff, dressed in breeches and gaiters, a bit of a dandy, a kind of 'Beau' Brummell. He exuded authority, although Old Ted Green doubted some of his farming practice. 'You can't learn farming from a book,' he said to Joe Woodman in the Old Inn over a pint. However, they both knew that Tom Dudley and his wife Freda were good employers, paying more than the odds in wages. Bill White, the jobbing builder, agreed, admitting that working for Tom was like 'a job in the Town'.

The War Agricultural Committee's machinery depot, 2 miles from Ayshon, had equipment that was hired out to the farms. It offered the pick of the tractors, etc, but the farmers had to wait their turn if they wanted to buy. This was no problem for Tom Dudley though. His Birmingham factory manufactured machinery that included agricultural implements. He had his own ways of getting a new Fordson tractor for Hawthorn Farm.

The day it arrived Harry Lock was harrowing some of the hill land with the pair of Suffolk horses, land broken up from pasture for potatoes. Ted Green was repairing a stone wall that enclosed a pasture where ewes and lambs grazed. Harry was a bit dubious about the field known as The Slad, about growing these particular

6 acres with Gladstone potatoes. Ted reminded him of the submarine menace during the First World War. 'Mind you,' he said 'the War Ag who ordered our Gaffer to plough The Slad is populated with some devious customers. Broken-down farmers, dealers, and yellow bellies, there to get out of the Army. I'm in favour of the ploughing up campaign. In the Bible it says "Break up your fallow land".'

In December, when the corn ricks were threshed, Tom spent a whole week at Ayshon, keeping an eye on the operators. He was fascinated by machinery and smiled to himself at what he called the primitive belt-driven threshing box, so different from the equipment at his factory. Every morning, as the hired tractor started the long belt turning the works and the corn began to pour into the sacks, Tom would be there watching the team at work.

'Just see that the wire netting around the stack is erected properly, Mark. We need to kill all the rats before they escape.'

'I'll keep a check on it,' the bailiff replied from the rick where he and a couple of land girls were pitching sheaves onto the machine. And boys on holiday from school would patrol that area between the rick and the wire netting, armed with rick pegs to kill the rats as they tried to escape.

'He's a stickler for little things like that,' Ted Green remarked to Joe Woodman as he carried a sheet of chaff to the barn.

Joe was pitching boltings of straw tied with two bands of twine to Harry Lock, who built the straw rick. Two Italian prisoners carried the sacks of wheat, each weighing 2¼ cwts, up the granary steps.

'Now Ted, how are you? You must have helped at a good many threshings in your time.' These words from the master of Hawthorn Farm prompted Ted to stand and think a while.

'Well, Sir, I be seventy on me next so it's a few years since I first went threshing. I used to carry the 2¼ cwt sacks comfortably then. Now it's all I can do to carry the empty sack. That and getting wet through ditching and draining is the cause of my rheumatics, you know. We thought then that we were immortal; still, there's a lot up in the churchyard who'd be glad of what I've got, that's certain.'

CHAPTER TWO

LAND GIRLS

In Ayshon the difference between Thomas Dudley's land girls, Ivy, Connie and Audrey, and the village girls soon became apparent. The war lingered on, the village school doubled its numbers with evacuees, and now the camps were full of American soldiers. Ivy and Connie, from north London, two sisters who had worked in printing before joining the Land Army, were not going to be seduced by the Yankee uniform and big talk of the fellows from the States. However, the glamour of those crepe-soled shoes and brass-adorned jackets, the men who seemed to have an endless supply of Camel cigarettes, money and nylons, bowled over some of the village girls.

Ted Green, that wise old countryman who had served in the First World War and had dilly-dallied with what he called The French Wenches, said to Mark Dale's wife, Mary, 'I be pleased that your two girls from London be keeping clear from trouble. They be street wise, and unfortunately that don't apply to our locals. The trouble is the village girls have never been no farther than the County Town.'

Mary smiled. 'I see your point, Ted. Ivy has a boyfriend in the Army while Connie's fellow is in the London Fire Brigade. They're not looking for anyone else.'

Ted then told Mary that he had been in the Old Inn the night before and one of the Yanks, as he called them, was spinning such a tale to one of the Smith girls. He continued, 'He said "You know my father owns a big estate in California, raises beef cattle, grows corn on several hundred acres, but I joined the colours." Joined the colours! And young Peggy Smith took it all in.'

The country village was unable to cater for the land girls on the same scale as the city did, with its cinemas, theatres and dancing.

Whist drives and dances had been held on occasions at Ayshon, especially towards Christmas when 'Fur and Feather' whist drives meant prizes of pheasants, hares and rabbits, but these country dances were quite different. The dance band from the next village provided the music in the village hall, an army hut heated by a coke stove; what amused the girls from the city was the row of chairs by the stove occupied by the old village dames all knitting. Knitting at a dance! The floor, wooden and worn, created clouds of dust as the couples danced. Village lads in competition with the brass-adorned GIs did a turn with the land girls.

But the GIs would entice their partners to the orchard outside with words that became familiar: 'Take a breather, Honey?'

Audrey Mosely, who had been Freda Dudley's hairdresser in the city, found that National Service on Tom Dudley's farm as a land girl suited both her and the wartime authorities. She was a blonde bombshell.

Bill White was the handyman-cum-builder on the farm who had rebuilt the stables. He lived with his wife in a neighbouring village. Audrey's figure, her soft, kind manner and that platinum blonde well-groomed hair under a snood set Bill thinking, dreaming of her as she fed the hens or milked the house cow for the Dudleys.

'Do you play darts?' he asked her one day as they sheltered in the barn from a storm.

'Yes, I used to play for a team at Solihull,' she replied.

Bill pondered, wondering whether he should ask her to join the team of villagers. 'Would you play for the team at the Old Inn?' he finally ventured.

'Yes, I can cycle there. What time?'

'Seven o'clock,' Bill replied.

The next evening Bill, in his Sunday Best, introduced Audrey to the locals. 'Oh, ah,' some said. 'You can pick 'em, can't you?' Bill paid for the drinks. Audrey hit double top at the right moment – and some said so did Bill!

Their friendship developed and they spent every night in the Snug at the Old Inn. (Bill and his wife had an invalid daughter which made it impossible for them ever to go out together.) No one speculated how the relationship progressed, but Bill confessed to his wife when she put a stop to his association with what she called his 'Fancy Woman'. And he admitted to me: 'Maybe I overstepped the mark.' What happened between him and Audrey after the darts matches, when they cycled home together, remains a secret. The searchlights criss-crossed the sky as the German bombers dropped their heavy ware 30 miles away on Birmingham. Bill gave me a knowing look as he recalled sheltering in Dudley's hay barn, adding: 'You got to keep your own council in a village.'

CHAPTER THREE

DOE BANK

From Ayshon the lane ran north and soon the county boundary was marked. It was here that policemen from Gloucestershire and Worcestershire would meet, in a kind of ritual. George Burford described it by saying: 'They swopped knives.' To be precise, they gave each other information gathered during the day. The meeting was usually at night.

About a mile further on, past where the Old Salt Way abutted the road, lies the hamlet of Doe Bank. The last place God made, George Burford said many times as he walked that road where the grass grew green up the middle. The horse traffic kept the limestone lane free of grass apart from the ribbons of green in the centre.

At Doe Bank stood a rather grand Victorian house, The Laurels, with 15 acres of hobby farm below. Cottages dating from about the same time as the house were built in a quadrangle surrounding a little grassy paddock. Here hens, chickens, geese and some goats competed for space with the children of the hamlet.

John and Jane Bushell were from the Black Country, where John was a successful solicitor. They had one daughter, Maud. They would come to the big house for weekends. Ted Green lived at Doe Bank too, with his mother and father. They occupied one of the spacious cottages in the quadrangle. Life at Doe Bank moved at a leisurely pace, and they all enjoyed it.

John Bushell was a generous man, he loved his gun and was often invited to Hawthorn Farm to the pheasant shoots in the woods. He did stutter, although that seems to have had little effect on his work as a solicitor as he was prosperous. He employed a cowman with a little herd of Shorthorns, a chauffeur who helped at haymaking, and a couple of maids who lived in when the family were away and made the butter, collected the eggs, and looked after the poultry. The place was a little palace in the wilds.

As time went on Ted Green left Doe Bank, John and Jane Bushell died, and Maud was left as the last of the family. Maud had been mother-smothered, it is true, and when the prospect of marriage came along her parents had overruled it. Maud suffered from the break-up of the romance, and she became a recluse. The firm of solicitors made her a ward of court and engaged a chap called Bob Cooper to live in. In the long run, maybe this was not a good move, but Bob at least made sure the bills were paid, with money from the solicitors, he looked after the garden, and he kept the house warm, but he and Maud saw little of each other. She went to bed most of the day and was up and about at night. Before Maud's parents died they had engaged a housekeeper – the chauffeur was ordered to take her on Sunday nights to Ayshon Chapel. The coal man, the milkman, and the travelling shop called at The Laurels, so Maud did have some company during the week. It was at that time too that Phil Grafton sometimes went to supper there, with his wife Mary. But things changed dramatically when the housekeeper died and Bob Cooper ruled.

Phil still visited Maud, feeling so sorry for her, and when the butcher brought the weekend joint Phil marvelled at the size of the leg of lamb, not to mention the slice of rump steak on the side of the plate.

'What's the steak for, Maud?' Phil was puzzled.

'Oh!' Maud replied, 'That's for Bob's supper.'

The mobile shop came with young Peter, who carried the order into the kitchen. Bob checked the provisions then said, 'You haven't brought the Body Mist.' It was then that Phil knew that half the stuff off the van was being flogged by Bob at the pub. When the solicitors were informed they said it was the best of a bad job – who else would stay with Maud? She had become a pathetic sight with only her cats as company. Generous with what money she could get from Bob she bought cat food for the folk in the hamlet and the village.

Phil noticed that the valuable paintings in the sitting-room were disappearing a few at a time.

'Where is the oil painting from over the fire place?' he asked.

Maud's answer was, 'Oh, Bob's put it away safe upstairs.'

Phil knew that travelling second-hand merchants had been to the door of The Laurels and Bob had sold these valuables in a trice. He also knew that every weekend Bob's divorced wife came by bus to Doe Bank, and that she returned to Worcester with big full shopping bags.

One Christmas Day when Phil visited The Laurels, he heard crying coming from behind the shutters of the bay window of the drawing-room.

'Where are you?' he called.

'I'm locked in the house. Bob's gone to the pub.'

Phil was able to get through the window and unbar the front door. He then went to see the Vicar.

'You're the first person to come here and not say that Maud should be put away,' the Vicar remarked.

'Of course she shouldn't,' Phil said, and the Vicar, knowing that Bob was on a good wicket, recognised the problem.

Maud soldiered on regardless at Doe Bank. She said the hamlet was named because of the multitude of rabbits on the hill, bucks and does. It was a mercy that Bob died before his generous employer, and Maud lived in the house she loved for another eighteen months before she too died there.

Henry Northway was another resident of Doe Bank. He was a door-to-door salesman, known as an outright in those days. One year, at the Evesholme Mop, Henry met Gladys Moreton, and soon 'twas said they were going steady.

Gladys was the daughter of Charles and Emma Moreton. Many of the men discharged from the Army after the Peace celebrations of 1919 had been unable to find employment; by the 1930s, disillusioned, they tramped the roads as nomads. These ex-soldiers took whatever temporary jobs they could find, and slept rough in barns and stables.

Charles Moreton was such a man. He came to Ayshon with his wife Emma, pea-picking on a neighbouring farm. With them was

Gladys, at that time a girl of sixteen. They took up their quarters in a building next to where a Hereford bull was chained, a bothy. Here the family stayed after the peas were picked and Charles worked on the farm. He joined a little gang of men hoeing the cabbages then picking sprouts. Charles was a very skilled worker on the land. How sad that his life had been wrecked by serving his country in the war.

Charles had married Emma, a gipsy girl, and the couple had wandered the length and breadth of England as temporary farm workers. The bothy proved to be the best place they had found since their wanderings started. Down near the railway line another farmer had an empty cottage known as Land Close. The Moretons moved in, and Charles finally had a permanent job. Gladys helped with the living costs, working as a domestic servant at a couple of the Ayshon houses. Just as her mother had always been clever with her gipsy tongue, so too was Gladys, a smooth talker but very hard working.

When Gladys met Henry, she told him that she was the daughter of a well-known doctor (of the same name) who practised in a nearby town. Whether he believed her or not is doubtful but Henry was seduced by her olive complexion and her black wavy hair; and she rode a motor bike.

They married and Henry and Gladys Northway lived in one of Miss Maud Bushell's cottages in that quadrangle at Doe Bank. Gladys worked on one of the farms there as cowgirl, milking, feeding, anything which needed doing, haymaking and harvest. She was better than any of the locals at working with animals and crops. Her father and mother finished their days at Land Close as pensioners.

Gladys, the driving force in the relationship with Henry Northway, became something to be reckoned with among the cottagers of Doe Bank. She kept goats in the little paddock where the cottages formed a quadrangle. The goats multiplied in numbers and strayed onto a neighbour's land. He was a military man, an ex-officer in a Guards regiment; he used his Army voice to threaten Gladys about the trespassing goats. But this was a young woman afraid of nobody, and she threatened to throw the man over the garden wall. Gladys knew just how far to go to keep within the law, but some neighbours were afraid of this 'Boadicea' who had settled among a few quiet country folk. Henry did visit the local pub but there were strict rules to be kept at the Northway household, where two boys and a girl now made up the family.

Henry was a successful salesman who gained promotion with his mail order firm. One evening, a chap who worked for a time at Hawthorn Farm saw Henry try to perform a feat at the bar of the inn which really defies description. He had been on his rounds and called at the pub for a drink and a snack. With a pork pie in one hand, he took mouthfuls of pie in between drinking a pint of cider and smoking a Woodbine cigarette. Henry was a success as a salesman but the locals were aghast at his manoeuvres between pork pie, cider and the Woodbine.

One hot summer evening Henry had had a hard day on his rounds and his car was at the garage being serviced. Gladys had given up the regular job milking a farmer's cows but had still been out that day too, helping with the haymaking. Without a car Henry did some local canvassing for orders on his bike. The sight of the local inn that hot dusty evening was too much for a thirsty man to resist. He propped his bike against the wall of the inn and went to the bar. He was not a heavy drinker, a couple of pints of cider was his limit. When Henry returned to his bike to ride the 1½ miles back to Doe Bank he found the tyres were flat. Maybe the hot sun had lifted the patches on the inner tubes. Tired and weary he pushed the bike to Doe Bank.

'Sorry to be late, Gladys. I've had a puncture and have had to push the bike home.' Little did Henry know that Gladys had seen his bike outside the pub.

'Ready for your dinner, Henry?'

'Too true,' Henry replied.

'Well, you will find it in the oven ready for you.' Opening the oven lid, Henry's eyes fell on a plate upon which were two valves with valve rubber attached from his bicycle.

'That's your dinner,' said Gladys with a laugh. Her husband dared not say a word. Gladys was able to box his ears like a mother to a child; he was under petticoat government.

Gladys was forever visiting auctions, buying brass and silver as her gipsy ancestors had done before her. She made money from jumble sales, and from going door to door buying second-hand furniture and antiques. She had an eye for a bargain. As the locals said, Gladys had by now got a fairish stocking. (They still talked of the old days when families kept their savings in a stocking.) Between what she had saved, worked for, and her dealings at the door, Gladys probably had more money than any of the cottagers of Doe Bank. Henry's widowed mother, who lived in South Gloucestershire, died at about this time. Henry, the only child, was left the whole of her small estate in her will. Meanwhile, Maud Bushell's chauffeur had left The Laurels, where he'd lived after Maud's death; the property had been empty for some years.

What Gladys Northway paid Maud, or Maud's estate, for this substantial property is anyone's guess. Gladys did the dealing with Henry's money. She could strike a hard bargain. Soon, the Northways moved in. The roof was in a bad way, leaking. Any other woman would have engaged a builder to repair it, but not this Boadicea. She ordered scaffolding, planks and poles, and stripped the roof herself, redoing it and making it weatherproof once more. In the living-room the paving slabs were uneven, broken and the floor was bad. Gladys put down a perfect parquet floor: it was not an imitation floor, but real oak blocks set in pitch.

The Northways lived at The Laurels for some years, but then the gipsy in Gladys urged her to move on. She needed no estate agent to sell this property; the spiel she rolled off about Oliver Cromwell, King Charles, and how the Civil War had raged outside her house was more than intriguing to prospective purchasers. The couple who bought it found it an oasis after the Birmingham suburbs where they had lived.

CHAPTER FOUR

ANOTHER ROMAN INVASION

Not since the Roman legions had ruled Ayshon and the Hill had such an influx of men from 'long-legged' Italy worked on the land. These Italian prisoners of war arrived in the village in the early 1940s. Their impact on farming and the village was a part of the revolution in agriculture.

Until then, staid men of the village had worked quietly, planting the crops, tending the farm animals, in much the same way as their fathers and grandfathers had done. But the Italians were so different; they sang as they worked, they laughed, and when a group of them got together the noise was not unlike a flock of starlings. Maybe Mussolini's conscripts were relieved to be away from the battlefields and found rural life, even in captivity, better than the heat and dust of the North African desert.

Camps were set up to house these men, dressed in their distinctive brown battledress marked with full moon shaped rings of white. A lorry took them every morning to work on the local farms.

Guiseppe and Pedro, both from the Naples area, came to my farm. They spoke just a few words of English but quickly learned. Communication was difficult at first but Pedro, who had been a farmer in Italy, growing olives and grapes, soon fitted into the farming practices of Worcestershire. When we think of Trade Unions and their control of labour, well, they had nothing on Guiseppe and Pedro. Every morning a council was held on that Army lorry as the men were allocated to farms in the area. Guiseppe told me what the prisoners would say.

'Where you work today? Oh, Mr Smith.'

The men then said, 'Him very good boss. Plenty cigarettes and cider. We do plenty work. Where you work? Mr Jones. Him bad boss, always swearing at us. Not too much work.'

Human nature dictates that men can be led but not driven.

The Italians' noisy chatter had an impact on the livestock of the farm. Horses laid back their ears, they would not stand still. This language, this exuberance, upset the horses, who were used only to the slow quiet speech of the old farm workers. Guiseppe was a handsome, dark-haired man, broadshouldered and strong, a natural comedian. Every day he and Pedro took Tommy, the liver chestnut cob, with a four-wheeled dray to the orchards, bringing back the fruit in the evening. As Guiseppe drove the cob down that half mile of country lane he would stand upright behind the shafts of the dray singing. A twentieth-century Roman charioteer. The horse, excited by the chattering of these southern Europeans, trotted and sometimes cantered for home. As the dray-load of fruit passed the cottages old men stood at their garden gates, school children cheered, a few looked shocked – shocked that these men, our enemies, were singing through the village.

Football was the prisoners' pastime at the camp. When he had learnt a little English, Guiseppe talked to me about it.

'You play football?' I said to this man, who reminded me of Primo Carnera the heavyweight boxer.

'No, Boss. My Mother very old, not possible to make another Guiseppe. When me dead, me always dead; and if I break my leg Mr Churchill will not give me another one.'

This man we called Joe thought a lot of his mother. Pedro was a married man with three children. The two Neapolitans asked me if they could live in a bothy at the farm. I fetched them with their things from the camp, signing a form which said: 'This day I have received the live bodies of Guiseppe Clarido and Pedro Peddalino.'

Soon after the two men took up residence in the bothy Pedro's eyes became fixed upon Nancy Pitcher. She flaunted herself at the village cross; a girl of twenty, she was the youngest of a big family. Guiseppe called her 'Temptation', with her short skirts and low-cut top. She worked at the jam factory in the nearby town. Pedro could be seen walking the lanes and fields of Ayshon with this young village Venus. Guiseppe was concerned, perhaps a little jealous of his fellow prisoner. 'You think what I think, Boss? Pedro and Nancy make love, and what will the village folk think?'

Within a few days one staunch Chapel Elder approached me. 'Your Italian prisoner I believe is keeping company with Nancy Pitcher.' I nodded. 'You should stop it, you know,' he replied.

I explained that Pedro did a good day's work for me and how he spent his evenings was his concern. Even so, 'keeping company', I mulled over in my mind, that's putting it mildly. There could be problems, I thought, if that silly young Nancy ended up 'in the family way', as it was generally known. Old Ted Green remarked, 'Wait until her's as old as me and she will be in everybody's way!'

Nancy had been around a bit with the factory workers and was probably wiser than her years; although sometimes appearing dim, she could not be described as innocent regarding the dangers of sex.

I usually went to town on Fridays to the bank for the wages and to do some shopping.

'Boss,' Guiseppe stood at the garage door with Pedro. 'You go Evesholme?'

'Yes, Joe.'

'Cigarettes from camp no good, similar smoking straw.' I nodded as he offered me half a crown. Oh, they did make some money making baskets from the brook-side willows. 'Boss, bring me some Players Please. Me plenty cigarettes, Boss, me plenty work.'

Pedro was reluctant to speak at first, but said in a quiet voice, 'Will you get me some Preservedis.'

Taken aback a bit I replied, 'I'll see.'

In town the purveyor of rubber goods always sold from under the counter, secretively. He was a little herbalist, known locally as 'the prevention officer'. He supplied Pedro's order. Whether it was right of me I don't know, but I think it protected Nancy from starting a child.

On another occasion Guiseppe winked and said in broken English, 'Alright for some, Boss. First Sebastian, now Pedro, what about Guiseppe?' Sebastian worked on a neighbouring farm where the farmer kept pigs. The farmer was an unattractive little man who smelt of the sty, but his wife was tall, slim, and attractive, with long auburn curls falling nicely onto the collar of her Harris tweed coat. She worked at a solicitor's office in town.

'What you think, Boss?' continued Guiseppe. 'You think Sebastian and Mrs Basset are lovers?'

I smiled but made no reply.

Now if ever there was an Italian prisoner who could be compared to the most handsome of film stars it was Sebastian: tall with sparkling brown eyes, wavy black hair, a row of teeth which, when he smiled, flashed white under a pencil thin moustache. As Nancy was Temptation to Pedro, so Mrs Basset was to Sebastian. One speculates, that's all.

After a time in the bothy Guiseppe managed to get hold of a bike. Some 6 miles away, where the men went for a hair cut, a group of prisoners rigged up frames and wheels, setting up their friends with bikes. On winter nights, when the German planes passed overhead en route for the Midlands, black-out restrictions declared that lights on a cycle should be dimmed. On one such night, Guiseppe, with a duly dimmed electric battery lamp, went to town. He had found a lady friend. On his way home as he came through a neighbouring village his cycle lamp had gone out completely. The village policeman happened to see him and called, 'Where's your light?'

Guiseppe replied, 'Finisho battery.'

Pedalling away with the policeman behind him, providing light from his own cycle lamp, Guiseppe reached the bothy breathless but out of danger.

As the war dragged on the day arrived when the Italian Army capitulated to the Allied Forces. What a day that was at Hawthorn Farm! Mark Dale the bailiff took his Italian labourers from the Army lorry every morning. He didn't billet prisoners on the farm as I did. As the news came through, Mark's men refused to work; their world had collapsed about them. Sitting in the stable with tears streaming down their sallow faces they remained subdued all day.

Mark tried to entice them to work and offered cigarettes, but there was no response from the remnants of Mussolini's Army. This may have been engineered on the transport lorry, but that day not a stroke of work was done by the prisoners. Guiseppe and Pedro, working for me, reacted in a less dramatic way; they just wanted to return to their country, a country now free from Fascism.

Later, Guiseppe came into the yard announcing, 'Boss, finish carboni.' The little range in the bothy had burnt all the coal. We always fetched coal from the wharf at the station yard. Roy, my tractor driver, used to take Tommy, the cob, in the dray and collect 5 cwt at a time. It was rationed. 'Just fetch some coal for the Italians,' I said when he came into the yard.

An hour later Roy arrived back with 5 cwt on the dray and began unloading it outside the bothy. The Italians had been in Britain for a couple of years and now understood English. Indeed, Pedro had become a quite fluent master of our language. Guiseppe found some words difficult, but he could understand when Roy and I were talking.

Roy, a great leg-puller and tease, looked at me as he shovelled the coal from the dray. He had that mischievous look in his eyes. I wondered what was afoot. Guiseppe was standing nearby. Giving me the weight ticket, Roy related how the man at the coal wharf had asked him whether the coal was for Mr Archer or for 'those blooming Eyeties'.

'I told him it was for the prisoners,' Roy continued. '"Well," the man at the wharf replied, "Get some out of the next truck, it's not such good coal in there."'

Guiseppe's arms went up in the air; he shouted so loud he could be heard for some distance: 'Anything is good enough for prisoners.' Then came a lot of cursing and swearing in Italian as he crossed himself, looking up to the heavens.

Roy winked at me, saying aside, 'There was only one truck of coal in the station yard, only one quality. I thought I'd make Guiseppe blow his top, and it worked!'

Things soon settled down at the bothy. Pedro, the farmer, grew aubergines, tomatoes, onions and peppers in the garden he dug next to their wartime home. Guiseppe would stand with arms akimbo, puffing smoke from his Players Please cigarette. Then he'd take a couple of mugs from the cupboard and turn the tap on the 4-gallon barrel of cider which had been delivered, filling his mug and one for Pedro. As he drank the wine of the West he would smack his lips and say,

'Multo bene, Boss, very good.'

Guiseppe was not so handy at basket-making as his fellow prisoners. He made a bit of money working in the cottage gardens of the widows of the village.

Every evening the fry-up in the bothy would fill the farmyard with the aroma of Italian cooking. Over the range the pan of potato *frite*, tomatoes, onions and spaghetti gave flavour to the meagre meat ration. (Rabbits were a plague in the Hill but what a benefit they were for the wartime kitchen. With snares Pedro would often catch what he called 'one of the coneys' and add it to the rations.)

There was one more strange rule observed by these men – they always shaved before eating their meal. Guiseppe reckoned that to shave after a meal made it so much easier for the razor to cut the chin.

CHAPTER FIVE

THE LAST OF THE WAGONERS

When Thomas Dudley farmed Hawthorn Farm he took advantage of his position as an important Birmingham industrialist. He had his finger on the pulse of wartime production, and rightly so. Producing in his factory heavy machinery for the war effort gave him the opportunity to mechanise the farm with the latest machinery of the day. Thomas Dudley's Fordson tractor was fitted with pneumatic tyres.

Fred bought a 1942 Standard Fordson for £140 new from the agents, but it was on spade lug wheels. That was a bonus on the Midland clay, but Thomas Dudley's men could haul his crops on the road on rubber wheels. He did also have two Suffolk geldings which did light work on the hill lands. Handsome they were, named Punch and Jack.

To haul crops from distant fields to the farmyard Fred depended on a mare named Pleasant and her son, Prince. They were a useful pair pulling the farm wagons. Roy, a strong sixteen-year-old village lad, drove Fred's Fordson and became a very good operator with a three-furrow cockshut plough. Roy was the youngest son of Ralph, who had worked with horses when Queen Victoria was on the throne.

There's no doubt that young Roy inherited some of his father's skill with horses. To see Roy driving Pleasant in the wagon shafts with Prince in front in traces was poetry in motion. With a leading rein on the trace horse he walked, he talked with his little team, and it seemed they knew what he said. Before the war when horses and men were thick on the ground Ralph had mowed and reaped with horses, changing the teams at dinner-time. Horses were returned, lathered with sweat, to the stable and replaced by fresh animals.

We hear a lot today about do-it-yourself shops. It's not new. Folk improvised during the war on the farm. Machinery had to be altered so that it could be pulled by the new tractors. The long pole on the mowing machine, which had borne down on the collars of the horses long since gone, was sawn off. Mowing had been hard work for horses when the 'old maids', horse flies, plagued them as the sun bore down on their backs and shoulders. The weight of that pole was sometimes painful as the collar pressed on their necks. Ralph called that part of their neck the crest, and often he was seen dressing their crests under the collar with soothing oils. Fred's Fordson pulled the old Bamford machine a little faster than the horses had done.

The short stub pole, as it was called, which was used to hitch the mower to the tractor, meant that the levers on the mowing machine were out of reach of the driver. Roy circled the standing ley while Fred sat on the iron seat of the mower and, with the levers, raised and dropped the bedding where the agitator knife chattered between the fingers cutting the grass.

Previously, the mowing was done by one man with two horses. Horses tire, they sweat, and they can get sore shoulders in the hay field but with the tractor Roy and Fred didn't have to change the teams at dinner-time. The tractor could work non-stop until twilight.

So Roy and Fred mowed that heavy ley of rye grass and broad leaf red clover in the Thurness field. But the tractor wasn't always better than the horse. Roy and Fred had to stop to sharpen the knives on the machine, and file the triangular blades; horses will tell you when the knife is blunt, but they had no such signal from the tractor. The tractor also had some problems at the corners, where previously the horses could make a sharp turn. When the corners of the uncut crop got difficult, Roy did a figure of eight with the tractor as Fred raised the fingers and the knife with the lever. Then he came in square with his tractor as Fred dropped the knife.

The crop in the Thurness field was heavy that summer and the broad red clover takes some making into hay suitable to crop. When they had finished the mowing, the following day had already dawned bright. Tom, Fred's stockman, as canny a man as he had ever known, advised Fred to turn the swaths. Fred had no swath turner; Mr Dudley's men were using theirs or he could have borrowed that one. There was no other way to turn the swaths than by hand. Tom and Fred, with young John, who had recently left school, circled the field turning a swath each to the blazing sun. The fodder turned from a dark green to a slatey grey as the sun did its work. Next day, John, with a horse rake, raked the hay into what was called walleys, or windrows. The rows of the clover hay were wide enough apart for a wagon and horses to travel between.

'I reckon it will be fit to carry on the wagons tomorrow,' Fred said optimistically to Tom.

He replied, 'Happen.' A good expression of his.

The next morning low clouds covered the hitherto blue sky. Tom picked up the half-made hay and said, 'It's gone back'. His expression meant that the brittle rye grass and clover had become tough.

The men turned the walleys all the morning and by tea-time Tom agreed, now the sun had come out, that 'It was fit to carry'. Roy brought Prince and Pleasant to the field from the stable a mile away. Three empty wagons were on the headland of the hay field. John then steered the two-horse team between the rows of hay and Roy with a short shuppick, or hay fork, began to take the pitchfuls from Tom and Fred. They used forks with long handles, called stales, and the long prongs of their shuppicks were known as grains.

There is an art to pitching hay, also in loading the wagons. After Roy had filled the bed of the wagon he called, 'Corners on the front', and Tom put his corner of hay skilfully on the edge of the overhanging raves of the wagon, and Fred did the same on his side. 'Now a pitchful between 'um,' Roy said, and that bound the corners together.

When the load was as high as the pitchers could pitch Tom said, 'Now Roy, fill the middle well in case of a storm.' They loaded all three wagons that evening. Roy took the first load, well roped, up the Groaten Road to the rickyard. He had to cross the main road to the Groaten, no mean feat with two horses. The road was fairly flat with just a slight incline but going over the railway bridge halfway home was a problem for the horses. Roy used to give them a rest, what he called blowings, by the Naits gateway. Somehow Prince, in traces, knew what was expected of him and was loathe to stand for long. With a flying start the horses and wagon ascended this obstacle. The iron-shod hooves of the pair of cart horses clattered to the top of the bridge. The wagons creaked, the overhanging hedge at the bottom before the road reached the railway company's hedge gleaned little wisps of hay from the load. At the top of the bridge over the little branch line Roy and his team stood a while, then Roy locked the nearside rear wheel with a heavy chain and put the heavy skid-pan under the iron tyre.

'Gee up,' Roy said to Prince, who walked, loose traced, in front of Pleasant. She sat back on her breeching, steadying the load down the slope past the grassy embankments known as The Batters. The chain was unhooked, the skid-pan, hot from its skate down the hill, and the locked wheel had melted the tar in a 6-inch mark.

The first load was unloaded onto a prepared staddle in the rickyard. A staddle was a platform of faggots of wood, mouldy hay and straw which kept the precious fodder off the damp ground. The evening star shone bright over the Cotswold Edge by the time Prince and Pleasant were taken back to Church Close. A little beginning had been made of the big hayrick.

Haymaking does differ from harvesting. During haymaking the loose hay is raked into walleys; at harvest, tidy sheaves are tossed to the loader leaving little behind. With haymaking it is pitching, and with harvesting it is tossing. 'Pitch' and 'Toss' were very real in those pre-hay-baling and combine-harvesting days.

The two loaded wagons stood overnight for Roy to haul next morning, while Tom the stockman suckled the calves on the nurse cows. Roy took the empty wagon back to the hayfield, riding side-saddle on Prince, the trace horse, with his heels in the traces. It was bait time when Fred, Tom, Roy and John began unloading the other wagons. The hay had settled overnight, and it would now be a hard task to unload the first wagon. Fred stripped to the waist. The rick was then only the height of their shoulders.

Fred had bought a useful mare named Bounce, so when the first load was on the rick John took Bounce in the shafts with another, empty, wagon to the field leaving the third wagon for Roy with Prince and Pleasant. Again the wagons were loaded, Roy taking them to the rickyard with his team.

'The weather looks black over Bill's Mother's,' Tom told them. 'I reckon we should put the hay into small cocks just in case it rains.'

So often, storms follow the Severn Vale, then split into two, one lot going along the Cotswold Edge and another storm following along the Malverns. These men were tucked in the Vale below Bredon, and the rain missed them. Tom and Fred found it easier pitching from the haycocks. Soon the wagons were loaded and Roy steered his team up the Groaten to the railway bridge.

'Yow be careful, Boy, coming up that bridge like the charge of the Light Brigade. You'll have them hosses with broken knees.' These words came mysteriously from under the bridge. It was Roy's Uncle Charlie, a ganger on the branch line. He was worried about his sixteen-year-old nephew. Roy looked over the bridge where Uncle Charlie was hammering the loose wedges into the chairs which held the railway lines.

''Tis no good coming up at walking pace, Uncle. I've got to take the incline at the trot.' And thirty-one times he did so, with load after load of hay, hauled to the rickyard over the bridge from that clover field.

As the rick got higher Fred, Tom, John and Roy put the elevator pole alongside. The hay was taken from the wagons with menacing-looking 'grabs', which Fred or Roy pushed into the load. John led Bounce alongside the rick hitched to a steel cable, which ran through pulleys to a gib overhanging the rick. Every grabful of hay was steered by Tom on the rick. 'Let go the painter,' he called. Then a rip-cord released each grabful as Tom had it dropped where he wanted. 'Let go the painter' – that's just something we will never know the meaning of.

This way of unloading was quicker and easier than throwing pitchfuls high to the growing stack. John and Bounce took the strain, then the forks or grabs had to be lowered by Bounce backing until the rope was slack. When the last load had been hauled John rode the horse rake and they pitched and loaded a wagon load of rakings.

When the haymaking was finished Tom pulled the loose hay from around the rick, which now resembled a country cottage. He thatched it with straw and withy rick pegs. He was proud of a job well done.

'We want some rain now for the aftermath clover to grow,' he said. These words that summer were in vain. The rain never came but, despite the drought, the clover still blossomed red in September. Once again Roy piloted his team over the railway bridge. It was a light crop of aftermath but, as Tom said, 'The cattle in winter would sooner eat that than their forefeet or a snowball.'

CHAPTER SIX

FROM SICKLE TO COMBINE

A sickle is a harvesting tool which goes back to antiquity. It has a serrated blade and was used by the harvesters, often women, to cut the corn. The method was to grab a handful of the standing corn in the left hand and cut it, not like a blow from a bagging hook but with a sawing action, leaving a long stubble. The bagging hook, or fagging hook, is used in conjunction with a wooden hook or crook known as a pickthank — thus the saying 'by hook or by crook'. When enough corn was cut to make a sheaf the pickthank gathered the cut material, which was then made into a sheaf with a straw band or bond made from enough of the cut corn to tie the sheaf.

Tom, the stockman, a man of many skills, was so good in the use of the bagging hook and the pickthank that he used to cut a road around the corn field making a way for the reaper/binder. He also cut patches of laid corn which the reaper/binder was unable to harvest.

It took the last war to bring women back to the harvest field to glean. Gleaning goes back to Biblical times, when Ruth gleaned the barley in the corn fields of Boaz. In Gloucestershire this gathering of the ears of corn left by the reaper is known as leasing. The gleaned corn was valuable in wartime to feed the hens of cottagers when everything was on ration. The gleaners didn't thresh the ears like their ancestors had done, the hens did the threshing, leaving the straw to litter the pig pen.

Tom, the stockman, remembered the harvesting at Hawthorn Farm when Victoria was on the throne. He spoke of the men who had allotments growing their acre of wheat and cutting it by hook and by crook. The sheaves were ricked in the Plough and Harrow yard in little ricks, then threshed by a threshing machine when the allotment holders combined to form a threshing gang.

Many times Tom described how he had taken off his shirt at dinner time soaked with sweat, putting it on a stook of corn to dry. Men didn't work bare backed and bare chested when Tom was young. The machine which cut, but did not tie, the sheaves took some of the hard work from harvesting. The sheaves were tied by hand, then put eight together to form a stook, a tent-shaped structure to shed off the storms. What a breakthrough it was when the reaper/binder was invented, which left the sheaves tidily tied with binder twine.

Soon after the Second World War the Major, who farmed Hawthorn Farm, hired a contractor to cut his corn with an early combine harvester. When we saw the Minneapolis Moline combine pulled by a tractor of the same name circling the Major's fields, some of our number thought it was the last word in harvesting. The corn was poured into sacks, which, when filled, slid down a chute onto the cut stubble.

That harvest was the last to be cut with the binder. Roy rode the Fordson around the Thurness field pulling the Massey Harris binder, which had been made for horse power. A.G. Street, in an article in the *Farmers Weekly*, had stated there was no need to cut a road around the headland of a harvest field for the tractor to travel. The idea was to cut the swath which the tractor had run over in the opposite direction with the fingers and blade of the machine pitched low. As Roy drove through the standing corn with Tom sitting on the binder like the captain of a ship, the sails of the machine coaching the standing corn to the blade, one wondered what thoughts he had. For a hundred years men had cut the headland under the hedge for the binder to have access – horses or tractors never trampled standing corn.

All went well that day until Roy stopped the Fordson the first time around the field. Tom dismounted from his high perch on the binder, while Roy pointed out a set of harrows which had been left since the seed had been planted, harrows now smothered by the standing wheat.

'Just in time I noticed it,' Roy said as he threw the harrows into the hedge bottom and the harvesting continued. After several circuits of the field it was decided to cut the corn trampled by the tractor under the hedge. The fingers were dipped with the knife close to the ground. Roy went slowly around the corn with the Fordson. The result was that little was lost, the machine had gathered the trampled wheat; it was the end of using the hook and crook to cut a road around the field.

It was Easter when the threshing machine came. It's well known that it requires at least seven men to form a threshing team. The spring was so dry, everything was tinder dry when the tractor came with a Fisher Humphries threshing machine, made at Pershore, just the other side of the Hill. The dust that day was indescribable and as the rick was half finished by dinner time, the corn ran well from the spouts on the machine to the sacks.

Fred had given a job to a chap off the road who had asked if he could help. His job was to carry the chaff a distance across the field and burn it. It was spring and the cattle were ready to graze the fields and chaff was not wanted.

By dinner time, everything was ablaze and there was no water for the fire brigade. The rick, the sacks of grain, the hay rick nearby, and the threshing machine were all burnt, and only the quickness of the tractor driver managed to rescue the tractor from the flames. It appeared that the tramp off the main road had brought some embers back to the rick on the sheet he used to carry the chaff. He had thrown the sheet under the partly threshed rick and the inevitable happened.

History does repeat itself, in farming as in village life. Tom, the stockman, told tales of carters in the horse age walking their neighbours' farms on Sunday afternoons. Why? you may ask. When a ploughman came to the village from somewhere else, his work would be under scrutiny. The furrows were examined to see if every bit of stubble was buried. It was much the same as with a young married woman being judged by the whiteness of her washing on Mondays.

The Major had harvested with the combine harvester and Fred decided to engage the contractor for his harvest. However, after the harvest at Hawthorn Farm the Major found himself with problems. As the straw lay in rows across the field the rain came down. The promised pick-up baler never arrived from the contractor.

Tom looked at the storm-damaged straw. He saw that the corn shed from the combine had sprouted and grown green in the swath of straw which had lost its golden look. The following week Harry Lock, Joe Woodman, Phil Grafton and Ted Green turned the straw with hay forks to dry in the wind. ''Twill do for litter in the yards, I suppose,' Joe Woodman said with some doubt in his voice. Major Sanderson was puzzled.

Ted Green suggested that the straw was stacked in the corner of the field. This meant pitching and loading loose straw. Was this how the harvest was going to end? The majority of the grain was in sacks and sold to a local merchant, but with loose straw to cope with, and damaged at that, the harvest had been so stressful.

Tom, an experienced worker who had seen so many harvests in his sixty years, told Fred of what he saw at Hawthorn Farm. He began, 'I'll tell you what, this yer menagerie that cut the Major's wheat unt all it's reported to be.'

'Why, Tom?' Fred asked. 'The Major's had his harvesting done in quick time.'

Tom then described what he had seen in Staites Furlong. Shed corn had grown in the swaths of cut straw, just like a lawn. 'That machine has wasted no end of grain. Joe Woodman showed me a sample from one of the sacks.'

'What was it like, Tom?' Fred was eager to know because he had booked the machine for the next harvest.

'The grains were a mixture of decent wheat and some green. It will heat if it's not dried,' Tom told him.

Fred wondered at this, realising that combine harvesting was labour saving, if the straw is baled, but as he and Tom stood in the rickyard their thoughts were of harvests past: the rhythm of pitching and loading sheaves from stooks; the pride Tom took in a well-built rick. They talked of sheaves maturing under the thatch in a rick of the hard grain, cleaned of tail corn and weed seed, which ran from the spouts of the threshing machine.

Something was going to be missing when the great contraption of metal replaced the farm wagons. Fred's thoughts were of how Tom had trained them to build the wagon loads of corn boat fashion. This meant building high at the front and rear of the load so that the pitchers tossed the sheaves to the lower load in the middle. This was loaded last. This would all be a memory when the combine gorged the grain. If the corn was laid by the weather, a great pick-up reel scratched it into the bowels of the machine. The thing seemed insensitive to nature. Sheaves were to be just history and when the folk at chapel sang 'We shall come rejoicing, bringing in the sheaves', it would sound hypocritical.

Fred remarked to Roy, who had driven the Fordson with the binder that last harvest, that he had seen a corncrake, or land raile, running in front of the binder; it was the last one to be seen in Ayshon.

'Bless the fellow,' was Tom's reply. 'They used to be common when I was a boy chap. But I'll tell you something; from what I have seen of the sample of wheat at Hawthorn Farm we shall never have a decent loaf of bread again. That's my opinion.'

The wheat planted in Big Thurness that autumn was a variety named Capelle, a soft wheat but high yielding. When at last the corn was fit for the combine harvester, August was past. George the contractor's excuse was that he had so many acres promised it made him late.

Fred had ordered some sacks from the railway company, sacks which held 2¼ cwt of wheat. These strong, hired sacks were similar to those that had contained grain for hundreds of years. Oh, yes, 2¾ cwt of wheat, 1½ cwt of oats, 2 cwt of barley, or 2¼ cwt and 14 lb of beans. These were the weights of the four bushel sacks.

By this harvest, Fred had pneumatic tyres on the Fordson tractor, and Roy came to the field with a two-wheeled trailer to pick up the sacks of wheat. Jack rode on the deck of the harvester, hooking sacks where the threshed grain poured from the machine. George's tractor forged ahead and as every sack was full and tied Jack slid it down the chute onto the stubble.

Tom untied one of the first sacks and took a handful of grains and sniffed it. Then he put some in his mouth and chewed the corn with his uneven teeth. 'It's no good for bread making,' he said. 'I told you we would never get a decent loaf of bread from these contraptions.'

'It will have to be dried,' Fred replied.

'Dried!' was Tom's response with a grin. 'It stinks of crow onions.' It was a well-known fact that only hard varieties of wheat were used for bread making.

As George soon cut 100 acres of the wheat, the straw lay in ever decreasing circles in rows around the field, and the sacks had to be loaded onto the trailer. The sacks of wheat were known as catch weights. Sometimes Jack tied a sack a little under the 2¼ cwt, other times, full to the brim, they would have weighed 2½ cwt. As Roy, Fred and Tom struggled with those sacks of corn Tom reminded them that taking a sack of corn from the threshing machine and wheeling it on a sack truck to the granary was so much easier. Lifting sacks lying on the stubble was a challenge to the strength of three men. The loads were taken to the barn, then loaded again on a lorry to go to the corn drier high on the Cotswolds.

'If this is labour saving, I'm a Dutchman,' Tom said after a day of loading and unloading 2¼ cwt sacks of wheat.

Major Sanderson at Hawthorn Farm was busy with harvest when George the contractor came to his farm. After one year with what Tom called 'That Contraption made of Tin', the Major had learnt one lesson about the sacks. He had used the heavy four bushel sacks the year before but this year he used smaller sacks that held a little over 1 cwt of wheat, sacks so much easier to lift than the four bushel ones.

Fashions in farming change very slowly, for hadn't A.G. Street written years before the war of the foolishness of four bushel sacks. The four bushel sacks are a memory, but a memory that had left behind old men with damaged backs, never designed to carry such weights.

The rain came down in torrents after harvest and the swaths of damaged straw sprouted green from the fallen grain again. What to do about it was a problem. Roy tried to plough the straw into the clay land, giving it some humus, but the plough clogged between the three mould-boards. Fisher Humphries of Pershore had made a single-furrow plough with a knife coulter instead of a disk coulter, a heavy implement. Fred borrowed such a plough from a neighbour, and Roy ploughed in the stubble and straw with a Fordson Major tractor, leaving the furrows to lax in the winter frosts. The combine harvester was creating many problems. Neatly thatched ricks of corn became a rarity in the countryside. Mechanisation derived from the factory took another step in ridding the country of something that had been just taken for granted for generations.

Fred's 2½-year-old cross-Hereford beef cattle had been sold at the Michaelmas Fair. He needed another eight or ten youngsters big enough to out-winter on the hill. It is often better to buy replacements at a genuine farm sale rather than at market. Fred took Roy in the car one Saturday to a little farm sale over in Warwickshire. The yearling cattle looked healthy. Eight young beasts came into the ring in the yard; they were described as bullocks. Fred bought them at what he thought was the right money.

In the yard when the cattle lorry was unloaded Tom was there having just finished suckling the calves on the nurse cows. 'They looks a useful bunch. But wait a minute,' he added, 'you have done summat, Frederick. There's two young bulls amongst um. Just something that can easily be missed.'

It was the following Wednesday when Gilbert Cresswell, the castrator, came over in his horse and trap from Tewkesbury way. The two bulls, separated from the six bullocks, were put in a loose box. Gilbert, an expert at gelding, castrated in the age-old way with hot irons and oils. He hotted his irons with a blow lamp and entered the loose box with Tom. One young bull made for the door, knocking the two men aside and into the yard. Oh, the job was completed but it was a late bit of surgery. I doubt if Tom ever forgot to remind his fellow workers of that Wednesday when Gilbert came with horse and trap to the farm.

Over at Hawthorn Farm Henry Lock did the mowing with a tractor mower operated by one man. These mowers were operated on the headland of the hay field by a cord from the tractor seat. Fred's old horse mower converted to a tractor machine took two men to operate it. Beside that, the machine was almost worn out. Next year he told Tom and Roy he would look out for a second-hand tractor mower. A farm sale advertised in the local paper included such a mower made by Bamford of Uttoxeter.

As the sale was the first week in May, Tom, the stockman, had turned out the young cattle from the yard. Some hay left in the ricks was needed for the suckling calves. 'How about a trip to Honeybourne?' Fred suggested to his stockman.

'What's on then, Frederick?' Tom queried.

'It's a farm sale and in the catalogue is a Bamford mower.'

Tom looked at the little farm staff in the barn, saying, 'Bamfords! I've used one of those machines with a couple of horses before any of you were born. I liked the Bamfords, higher geared than some makes.'

Fred and the stockman drove in the old Austin 12 to Honeybourne, a place with two churches and a railway junction, about 12 miles from Ayshon. The cattle and the sheep were sold first by the Evesholme auctioneer. This old farmer had farmed that heavy clay land for sixty years. Now on two sticks, he pottered around with his single daughter. The sale was going to be painful for the man as his only son had been killed in the war.

'A pretty useful lot of six half-bred Hereford cattle, Sir,' Tom said to the farmer as they stood alongside the ring, made from field gates in the rickyard. Dealers, farmers, marked their purchases and the work of a lifetime melted away like butter in the sun.

'Now for the implements, gentlemen,' the auctioneer called out in a hurry. Lot number 1 was a heap of scrap iron, old ploughs, broken harrows, which were bought by a scrap-iron dealer, men Tom called scrap-iron jacks. One was very conscious of the wind of change when a good reaper/binder went for a few pounds, to be followed by a horse rake bought by the scrap-iron men. Mechanisation was happening by leaps and bounds. Tools of the past were sold cheaply.

The farmer's tractor and plough made a fair price and Fred was waiting for lot number 65, the tractor-drawn mower. Tom had vetted the machine carefully for wear and tear. Fred bought it for £30 and arranged with the man who took his cattle and sheep to market to deliver it on one of his lorries.

Away from the main implements, five farm wagons stood in a row. The names of their previous owners were painted on the front board below the fore ladder. They gleamed in the May sunshine, bright yellow with red wheels, blue and gold. Here was a sight we would never see again. Tom looked around the wagons; some were narrow-wheeled, others broad-wheeled. He said someone had looked after those vehicles.

Honeybourne, Fred wondered; it was here Joseph Arch addressed the farm labourers about 1900. He spoke from a wagon. Harry Bailey, who Fred used to work for, had listened to this man who tried to organise an agricultural labourers' union. Words came to Fred on the day when the pitching of sheaves became history: 'Where once the broad-wheeled wagon lumbered in, Now we have a contraption made of tin.'

The wagons did lumber in; now Tom Higgins the blacksmith was making harvest trolleys from the chassis of old lorries. Everything moved on pneumatic tyres, moving faster behind the tractors. When the auctioneers came to the wagons few people showed an interest. 'Now come on gentlemen, let's have a start for these well-maintained wagons. Make me a bid.' Silence.

'These wagons, gentlemen, can be adapted with tow bars for your tractors. Give me a start.' No one spoke.

Then a scrap-iron dealer said, 'Sir. If we can burn them where they stand and recover the scrap metal we will give you £5 for the lot.'

The auctioneer had no option but to accept the bid. Everything had to be sold.

A caterer who had his stall in the barn was busy selling ham sandwiches, and some of the farmers were drinking whisky. 'I could do with a drop of cider,' Tom said to Fred and his wishes were granted.

Out in the field where the wagons stood, two men were setting fire to the work of a craftsman. Bales of straw were alight. Tomorrow the scrap men would collect the iron work. As the smoke wafted across the field to the Cotswold Edge, Tom sat on a bale of straw. Fred noticed tears running down his face. He said, 'Ah, years ago Joseph Chandler of Ayshon made wagons for £40 each. There's several sorts of seasoned wood in one of those.'

Fred started up the old Austin, feeling sorry that the old stockman had had to witness what he called vandalism when the wagons burned.

Tom had seen four men in line with scythes mowing barley on Hawthorn Farm before the First World War. It was quiet harvesting then, just the swish of the scythe blades. Then the grating noise of the rubber when the men whetted their tools. 'I never thought I should live to see good wagons burnt just for the scrap metal.'

When Fred and Tom arrived home it was past tea-time. Roy had put the milking cows in the long shed and the calves had had their evening milk. Tom's final words as he went to his thatched cottage were, 'I've told you before, we shall never again have any decent bread now the corn is cut by that combine contraption. Sheaves used to mellow in the ricks.'

CHAPTER SEVEN

HAWTHORN FARM BECOMES GRADE 'A'

So much improvement had been achieved at Hawthorn Farm, both through Mark Dale's management and Thomas Dudley's money, that the War Agricultural Committee upgraded the holding to a Grade 'A' farm. Mark was obviously proud of the fact when he announced the news in the Old Inn. 'That means drinks all round,' one wag remarked. Sipping his whisky and soda, Mark looked a bit taller than usual in his smart cavalry twill breeches and his gaiters, the typical leather patches on the elbows of the Harris tweed jacket.

'What happened up in the Langit, Master Dale?' my cowman said with a smile. 'Were you trying to drive the tractor through The Roughs towards Harry Lock's house, or did you fall asleep at the wheel?' As the cider drinkers laughed at the bailiff, they probably all knew what had taken place on that hilly field below the potato land. 'Come on now, Master Dale, let's hear the truth.'

'Well,' Mark replied, 'it could have been nasty. I was bringing a load of potatoes down the hill with the Fordson when the tractor and trailer jack-knifed. Yes, I did finish up on The Roughs. Now you chaps, fill your glasses and wish me luck as bailiff on a Grade "A" farm.' Amid cheering, the village oracles called out, 'Bless the bailiff, Mr Dale.'

Despite the little mishaps Mark Dale had as the bailiff of Hawthorn Farm his boss, Thomas Dudley, made a handsome profit both from the corn and the fruit. Trees which had never been pruned or fertilised responded to the treatment, producing fruit never before seen at The Hawthorns. In wartime a ready sale was certain as the imports from Europe had dried up. Every apple more than 2½ inches in diameter commanded the top price, regardless of variety. The price of pears was controlled and the Comice variety sold at a premium.

The orchard known as the Bank Piece had so many varieties. Harry Lock, described by old Ted Green as a slippery customer, a know-all, accompanied Thomas Dudley around the Bank Piece, reeling off a long list of names. One pear tree he called the Belle of Brussels was noted by Mr Dudley, but next year Harry gave it another name. Tom Dudley kept a list and discovered that, if Lock didn't know what name to give to the fruit, then he just made one up. Mark Dale trusted the whole gang of wartime workers, except Harry Lock. He must be credited for the way he handled this swarthy diddicoy.

Every Sunday afternoon during the last summer of the war Tom Dudley and his wife Freda circled the lanes of the village in their Governess car. Freda, pretty and petite with her hair immaculately waved and groomed by Audrey Mosely, Tom in a fawn Cotswold tweed suit sitting by the door of the car behind Freda. The cane whip in a holder on the mudguards was used only to wave at the old villagers as he passed their cottages. Was this man with the handsome, friendly manner, the new Squire? The fact was that Tom Dudley, born in Solihull and the owner of large factories in the Midlands, was more than Squire. He and his wife were benefactors to the community in wartime Britain. As Ted Green said, 'He's one of us.' Some Sundays the Dudleys went to Evensong at the church; not to enter by the little door through which the old Squire had approached his pew, but to sit at the back, unpretentious, humble folk from the city.

Bill White, the handyman of the farm, had only been exempt from military service because on registration his job description was 'farm mechanic and maintenance man' – a reserved occupation. He could mend a wagon, a plough, or a mowing machine, he could build walls and reconstruct stables and cowsheds. He was a valuable asset to Hawthorn Farm.

The flight of steps from the drive to Tudor House had become dangerous through neglect. Tom Dudley instructed Bill to build a tasteful entrance to his front door, using Cotswold stone. Bill ordered the stone and the cement, and he and Mark planned a wide flight of steps with handrails. Ted Green was to help too; he was what Bill described as his 'Stiff Un' (labourer). Halfway through the job a fellow from the Labour Exchange approached the men.

'Now look here,' he said to Bill, 'you are exempt from military service to work in agriculture. What's the meaning of this?'

Bill told the officer, 'Go and see Mr Dale.'

Mark Dale rang Tom Dudley at his Birmingham office; Mark was in a panic. In his usual laid-back way Tom responded, 'That's okay Mark, leave it to me. I'll deal with the man from the Exchange.'

The letter Tom Dudley wrote settled the affair; no more was heard about the problem with the steps. He had a way with words, a way with people, no one from some little office, not even the Labour Exchange, was going to tell this industrialist, who was producing so much for the war effort, what to do!

There was a great sense of relief when the war ended first in Europe, then in the Far East. Soon the Italian prisoners returned home. They were missed on the farm. A quietness settled over the fields. The land girls, too, went back to city life, apart from the few who married and stayed in the village, and labour was short. The War Agricultural Committee became more of an advisory service. Its machinery department, by contract work, filled the gap left by the workers now gone. The compulsory ploughing-up of pasture ended. Shortages remained but the urgency to produce more and more from the land was no longer so necessary.

When the servicemen who had worked on the land returned, it was not to the hard, back-breaking jobs they had left. Seeing the world had given them ideas of a new life. Modern conveniences and small gardens attracted them to the new council houses, and inside jobs, sheltered from the vagaries of the weather, in air-conditioned factories and offices, enticed them to workplaces in the city. The five-day week appealed too. At first, company transport picked up these men from the village and returned them in the evening. The money they saved soon bought a second-hand car and weekends at the sea-side or in the country. This was a Utopia never dreamt of before 1939.

I met such a man, who before the war and in fact during the war had worked on the land. Arthur plodded those endless rows of sprouts and peas behind a horse. Day after day he horse-hoed, he drilled, he cultivated the strawberries, the blackcurrants, on a neighbouring farm. The money, the hours worked in a factory tempted him. No more wet shirts or aching sore feet, he thought, 'I'll have a go.'

'How's life, Arthur?' I greeted him.

'Great,' he replied. 'If the bosses made me work twice as hard I'd not complain, and there's a canteen at lunch-time. No more standing under a hedge with bread and cheese.'

But looking at Arthur, a man now fifty years old, there was something missing. His rosy cheeks were gone, his face had a gaunt expression. The agile man I knew had been transformed. The muscles of his arms and legs were flabby, and there was a definite beer belly. So this was the five-day week, the transport to and from work! Arthur died in six months. It proved a point to me: workers on the land don't take kindly to the artificial climate of the factory. Men in the factory who begin their working life that way are acclimatized to the indoors.

Soon the farms took on this factory attitude, with big machines, air-conditioned tractors, sprays killing insects and weeds. Like a creeping paralysis the machines took over the work of country men.

At Hawthorn Farm, depleted by the loss of labour, Thomas Dudley knew that the bonanza of good prices for the fruit in his orchards would be over when imports from the continent returned. He had plans for his orchards to be grubbed up and more corn planted instead.

His dairy herd had become a feature of farming at Hawthorn Farm. The Red Shorthorns were served by a White Shorthorn bull, producing strawberry roan calves. Every heifer calf was kept for replacements, and soon he had a sizeable bunch of roan heifers, all TB tested. What a herd for milk production! And what a picture in his meadows by the village street! His flock of Kerry Hill sheep bought from Radnorshire ran with Suffolk rams on the Hill.

Up on the plain above the village where the beech trees grew among the gorse Tom Dudley had plans when the war was over to build a house overlooking the Vale and the Cotswolds. In fact, the site had been levelled all ready for the building. Then the foundations were laid; it was an exciting time for him and Freda, and the people of the village, for whom he cared so much, shared the anticipation. Then tragedy struck. Tom Dudley, at a board meeting where he chaired the company, suffered a heart attack and dropped dead like a stone. The whole village was deeply saddened. Mark and his wife, Mary, were absolutely nonplussed. The new house was never built. Mark found another job. Hawthorn Farm was up for sale. It was the end of an era.

CHAPTER EIGHT

New Farmers at Hawthorn Farm

It was a sad day at Hawthorn Farm when the live- and deadstock came under the hammer of the local auctioneers. Thomas Dudley had spent wisely, bringing a new look to the land under the Hill. Mark Dale had made the mistakes of a young man but basically, as bailiff to the Midland industrialist, he had done a good job. Mark had an intuitiveness that, without driving his little gang of men and women, had achieved what Thomas Dudley had aimed for, a happy workforce, a productive farm.

The Italian prisoners had returned to their country, and most of the land girls had gone back to the city. Audrey Mosely, who had left a hairdressing salon in the Midlands to be Freda Dudley's hairdresser, stayed in the village. The city girl who had spent the war years rearing calves, mucking out the cowsheds, playing darts at the Old Inn, having a fling with Bill White, just couldn't tear herself away from the country life. She bought a cottage and drove to the nearby town of Evesholme and opened a hairdressing salon there.

The sale at Hawthorn Farm was distressing for Freda. Her husband had gone to such lengths to build up the herd of dairy cows and the flock of sheep. She returned to Sutton Coldfield, leaving Mark Dale to assist the auctioneers in their description of the various lots and the farm animals.

Audrey Mosely was in tears when the roan heifers she had reared as calves went into the ring. They were almost old enough for breeding and she knew that Mr Dudley had been proud of them.

The two Suffolk geldings with gleaming liver chestnut coats, groomed by old Ted Green, were a picture in the August sunshine. They went to a local farmer. Harry Lock, that wily half-diddicoy who rented land adjoining Hawthorn Farm and lived in The Roughs, bought some of the Kerry Hill ewes for breeding. Ted Green said aside to Joe Woodman, 'Where's the new farmer? They says he's an Army major.'

'Too true,' Joe replied. 'That's him standing over near the auctioneer.'

Ted sighed. 'I've never worked for a military man. I suppose he will call us by our surnames. He's bought that little cob which pulled the Gaffer's Governess car. I believe that's for his daughter to ride. That's Jean standing by her mother, the blonde piece with the long cigarette holder.'

Joe then said, 'I don't think the Major will buy much of Mr Dudley's farm stock. They tell me he's going all modern with tractors. There's a big Country Crawler coming here at Michaelmas when he takes over. Phil Grafton, that young chap who used to be under-gardener at Tudor House, is going to be tractor driver.'

As Joe Woodman and Ted Green drained the last dregs of cider from their crock pots in the Old Inn they were wondering how things would change at Hawthorn Farm.

'He seems a decent chap, Joe.'

'Aye, Ted, I didn't catch just what you said.' The forester gamekeeper had been deaf since serving in the artillery in the First World War.

'Seems a decent chap,' Ted repeated. 'But you have been in the Army, you know how officers can be.' Ted then recalled the old Brigadier, who had died recently at the age of ninety-six. 'There's a Brass Hat for you mind,' he went on. 'A Boer War veteran, Horse Artillery, as hard as the Devil's back teeth.'

Joe then recounted how the Brigadier had started a local branch of the British Legion and had 'marched us up to the War Memorial with medals dangling like martingales on a horse, and those who could wore bowler hats. "I congratulate you, my men, on a very

smart turnout." Those were his words. I reckon we were more like
the awkward squad! The war came then and the LDV, Local Defence
Volunteers. The Brigadier was an old man but he was up on the
plain on Little Hill leading the company with his 12-bore gun
ready to shoot anyone who didn't answer to "Who goes there?".'

'Yes,' Ted replied. 'I joined with our old chap's muzzle loader,
then, of course, we had rifles when it became the Home Guard.
Mind you we shot a few rabbits at dusk when they came out to
graze by the gorse bushes.'

'Young Dan Coombes who milked that Shorthorn herd for Master
Evans . . . he had a number to milk with the machine . . .'

'Didn't he have a land girl to help, a wench from the Black
Country, Ethel by name?' interrupted Ted.

Joe said, 'Aye, I remember there was some trouble when the
Gaffer saw her standing by when the bull was serving a cow.'

Ted laughed. 'As if her didn't know how many beans make five.
Bist a gwan to try another pint you?'

'Just a half,' Joe answered. 'But what about young Dan and the
Home Guard! 'Tis like this. I know young Dan and his tricks in the
hayloft along of Ethel, how he chased her, but he worked long
hours, especially at haymaking. The brigadier, meeting him in the
road, never pulled his punches: "Coombes," he called, "I never see
you along with the company on the Hill." Now young Dan was a
bit slow in speech, brought his Cotswold accent with him. He
moved slow at work but what a worker! Ast ever seen him unload a
load of hay? Forkfuls like young ricks.

'I was telling you about his reply to the Brigadier. "Aye, I might
have a walk up one night and join my mates." "To hell with you,
Coombes," the Brigadier exploded. "That's not the spirit man . . . 'I
might have a walk up one night!' . . . I've seen men shot for
insubordination, or tied to the wheel of a gun carriage." The fact was,
Dan had registered for military service but being cowman to Mr
Evans he was in a reserved occupation, although he did join the Home
Guard. It was rifle inspection on the Sunday morning parade on the
Hill. The rank and file in the main were smart in their uniforms with

their rifles fit for inspection. When the Brigadier came to Dan Coombes he squinted up the rifled barrel through his pince-nez spectacles and detected something obstructing his vision. As he took a second look, a spider crawled out at the breech. "Are you breeding livestock, Coombes? For God's sake man, clean your rifle. A spider up the barrel! Keep to those cows tails, you will never make a soldier."'

Joe pondered a while; he and Ted reminisced. 'I don't think we've got anything to worry about over the Major. He's a different kettle of fish. But the Brigadier was good to us in the Legion if we needed help, but he, like Churchill, was in his element when a war was raging.'

It was Michaelmas Day the first year after the war ended when Major Frank Sanderson moved to Hawthorn Farm. He had bought the 350 acres, the farmhouse, and a house in The Roughs previously occupied by Harry Lock, for £27,000. The Major, everybody called him the Major, was a smart, upright man in his late thirties. Around the farm he could be seen in old battledress, but at market and at the Old Inn where he supped his whisky, delicate tweeds gave him that film star look. Oh, he was handsome. His wife, Lynda Sanderson, treated the village folk with some suspicion, but he bent over backwards to gain the affection of the people. He had served

with distinction in the Intelligence Corps during the war, and was an easy-going character. He took advice from Phil Grafton, the tractor driver, and most of all from that doubtful character Harry Lock.

Harry lived in The Roughs in a cottage among the hawthorn and brambles where Thomas Dudley had planted rhododendrons in that acid soil on the hill. It was a great pity that Mark Dale left the village after the death of Thomas Dudley. The young man trained in agriculture at Cirencester had proved himself to Thomas Dudley for his expertise in modern farming. Above all, he was a great judge of men's character and had weighed up Harry Lock to a tee. Harry kept his place under the bailiff.

Phil Grafton persuaded the Major to buy the massive Crawler tractor and the four-furrow plough. Harry Lock rode around the farm with the Suffolk horse in the shafts pulling the pneumatic-tyred farm cart. He used the vehicle to pick up feeding stuffs from Hawthorn Farm to take to The Roughs for his sheep and pigs.

The Roughs was an ideal spot for outdoor pigs. Hundreds of yards of wire netting encircled this area of land. The Major bought Wessex saddleback gilts and a Large White boar. In the years after the war the sheeted pigs were in demand at the markets. The young pigs grew to eight weeks and were then taken off to the market. The Major was generous with feeding stuffs, and loads of pig nuts came to Hawthorn Farm. Harry Lock's pigs in his rented buildings lived well on pig nuts while the Major's pigs were often short of food.

The sows and their litters did a good job clearing the brambles in The Roughs. They farrowed out of doors, one of the Major's ideas which worked. The eight-week-old weaners should have been fed on the rations bought for them but more and more food found its way onto Harry Lock's cart and into his piggery. The Major trusted the smooth-tongued Lock and Phil Grafton with his Crawler tractor.

One hears so much of farming being less labour intensive today than when men were plentiful and wages were low. It seemed that the Major, with his purchase of a big Crawler tractor, had in a way bought a cannon to kill a fly. A couple of acres of marrow stem kale in the Langit was planted for winter fodder, feed for the bullocks in the yard at Hawthorn Farm. Every morning Phil Grafton travelled the lane to the Langit with the Crawler tractor, pulling a trailer not much bigger than a car trailer. He was cutting kale in the field and transporting it to the cattle yard; a pony could have pulled the little load. Phil steered the giant with two levers. It belched smoke from the paraffin, and marked the tarmac in the lane. Phil, an exhibitionist, would shut off the ignition when he passed the villagers, then turn it on quickly. The engine would respond with a couple of explosions louder than a 12-bore gun. Meanwhile, where was Lock and his horse and cart? That is a question.

The uneconomic exploits on the Major's farm began to tell. The waste that winter in fuel, time and damage to the road was, in actual fact, money thrown away.

CHAPTER NINE

LOW CHURCHMAN
THE REVEREND NORTON

In the village, at church, on the cricket field, we all loved the new owner of Hawthorn Farm. It hurt to see a real gentleman being exploited. Lynda, Frank's wife, trusted neither Harry Lock nor Phil Grafton. She tried her best to get rid of Lock but the Major was always adamant about his workmen. Mrs Sanderson wasn't Women's Institute or Mothers' Union material. As old Ted Green said to Bill White, 'Her's above such organisations.'

Lynda was also very dubious about the Vicar's activities. The Revd Norton was an Ecumenical Evangelical, and didn't tolerate bowing and scraping at the altar. The Major still attended church; Lynda did too, but under protest and she hated Norton's insistence on shaking hands heartily with every parishioner after the service. 'The whole place', she said, 'has become completely Non-Conformist.'

The climax of the rift between Lynda and the Vicar came when Audrey Mosely went on holiday. She arranged for Patience Byrd to stay at her bungalow to look after the dog for a fortnight. Every evening during Audrey's absence the Vicar's car stood in the drive of the bungalow until midnight. Lynda Sanderson made up her mind to get to the bottom of this scandal, which threatened to rock the village. She phoned Revd Norton. 'Hello. That *is* the Vicar I am speaking to?'

'Yes,' he answered. 'Can I help you, Mrs Sanderson?'

'It's like this, Vicar. Your stay every evening until midnight at the bungalow is causing a lot of talk in the parish. Can you tell me why you are with Patience until that hour? It is said you are practising faith healing.'

The Vicar's response to the Major's wife has never been understood to this day. 'Oh, Mrs Sanderson, I have to go to the bungalow every night while Audrey Mosely is on holiday and Patience is looking after the place to wind up the clock.'

'To wind up the clock, Vicar! I've heard affairs called various things but never winding up the clock. If that's it, Vicar, you can count me out as a member of your congregation at least until you and Patience stop winding up the clock at midnight.'

One night in the Old Inn, Revd Norton was the topic of conversation between Ted Green, Joe Woodman and Bill White. (Between them the three countrymen could have written a newsletter about the goings on in Ayshon.) 'He's a faith healer,' Bill White said.

'Oh yes,' Ted replied. 'I know he and Patience Byrd be up to some capers, laying on of hands.'

Bill, a natural wag, chortled, 'Yes, but where *does* he lay his hands with Patience, as works at the Old Folks' Home. Of course,' Bill continued, 'Parsons and Gentry can get away with their bits on the side.' (Bill himself was still smarting over the pain he had suffered over his relationship with Audrey Mosely. 'No one will ever know the truth about her and me. Think what you like.')

'Gossip's a terrible thing, Bill,' was Ted's reaction as he called for three pints at the bar.

Joe Woodman was a chap who liked to think the best of his friends and neighbours. Although he admitted that the Vicar had some strange ways, he could still set some good points on him. 'You know the scandal at the Telephone Exchange, that Agnes was more than friendly with the copper,' he said. 'Well, we know why he spent evenings there – it was on purpose to listen to the phone calls. No one of any sense says anything private over the phone or it's known by the police. He's not going there any more, so I hear, and Agnes is lonely, can't sleep at nights. She's had a hard life. Now Revd Norton, the Vicar, is a sort of One Man Samaritan. When Agnes can't sleep she rings him up regardless of the time, even in the small hours of the morning.'

'What for, Joe?' Ted said with a surprised look.

'I'm telling you. The Vicar's a Good Samaritan. His voice over the phone talking to Agnes acts like a tranquilliser; soon Agnes is asleep.'

Ted and Bill listened while Joe described how Agnes and Patience lapped up every word of the Vicar's sermons as they sat transfixed in the front pew of the church.

Revd Norton had a following among the young folk at church too. He and Patience organised meetings known as squashes. Bill White described the get-togethers as Ping-Pong and Orange Squash – and no one in Ayshon ever discovered where that term came from.

CHAPTER TEN

HAWTHORN FARM
BECOMES GRADE 'B'

The Major wondered at times what sort of life he had let himself in for after the security of the Army. Lynda was unhappy at Hawthorn Farm because of the situation with Revd Norton, but Major Frank Sanderson still attended church though he decided not to take office as churchwarden.

The Major's farming was sometimes a disappointment. The fruit trees which had been such a money spinner for Thomas Dudley during the war still bore the crops, but because of the cheap foreign imports it sometimes wasn't worth picking the apples and plums. The War Agricultural Committee was no longer insisting on their ploughing-up campaign, but still listed farms as A, B, and C categories.

With the decline in crops at Hawthorn Farm the Committee decided to list it as a 'B' farm. Lynda Sanderson was livid at the news. She sent for the District Officer and the local representative to give an explanation. The two men were invited into what Lynda called the 'drawing-room' at Hawthorn Farm, a room full of Georgian furniture from her ancestral home in Worcestershire. A decanter of sherry and some biscuits were on the mahogany table, and the men were invited to sit and have a morning drink with Lynda. She was looking severe to say the least. Her cigarette holder appeared to be longer than ever as smoke from her Turkish cigarette eddied around the room giving off its exotic and foreign perfume.

She began. 'Tell me why you have downgraded our farm. My husband has only been here just over a year. You pen-pushing

bureaucrats don't know "A" from a bull's foot, coming here with your posh car.'

'Hang on, Mrs Sanderson. We are not complaining about the running of the farm. We know the hill land is difficult land. The farm is a Grade "B" farm simply because of the layout.'

Mrs Sanderson was not convinced. She showed the men to the door, threatening them that next time it was to be Grade 'A' or she would be in touch with the Minister of Agriculture. But the Major was not particularly worried. The War Ag was now more of an advisory committee. He was decisive enough over policy, but still he relied too much on Harry Lock.

The pheasants in The Roughs were scarce when the Major and his friends had the last shoot of the season. Someone advised him to stock the woodland with young guinea fowl; whose idea it was to loose the young birds in The Roughs is unknown. It may have been Harry Lock's. . . . When the birds came, the Major expected them to roost in the high trees away from predators, ready for the next shooting season. It is said that foxes cleared the woods of the fowl, but nothing was ever proved.

When the fruit trade had become a shadow of what it had been during the war the Major decided to sell some elm trees along the side of a hillside lane for cash. It happened that an American lady, named Janet Maxwell, had bought a field next to the Major's farm. Never had the village of Ayshon seen such a lady. She was a middle-aged free spirit, with an accent of the Deep South, who helped to rehabilitate prisoners on release and befriended gipsies who camped on her field. She had arrived with a Welshman, Taffy Edwards, and taken up residence in a cottage near the Old Inn. This wealthy widow had lived for a while in a commune in the Cotswolds. She had given Taffy Edwards the job of finding a couple of men to fell the Major's elms and, with a circular saw, to cut the branches into firewood logs. Taffy was to drive a lorry and deliver the firewood to homes in the district.

The men employed by Taffy had little idea of how to fell timber. The first two elms of the Major's landed not in the field but across the lane. Worse was to come. A giant elm in an orchard adjoining the churchyard had a heavy bough hanging over the boundary. Taffy was warned by Ted Green, who himself was handy with axe and saw. 'Now young Taffy, that bough will pull the tree over the fence. It would be best if you cut it off before you fell the trunk.'

'My men are experienced, Ted; there's no danger,' Taffy assured him. Taffy had a light rubber-tyred tractor. His men fixed a wagon rope on to the tree then on to the tractor. The chain saw was almost through the trunk when, just as Ted had forecast, the whole elm, with the heavy bough, fell across the churchyard. The rope was useless; it broke. Headstones were smashed as the tree fell, and the graveyard was covered with branches, twigs and leaves. At that moment, Janet Maxwell arrived with Revd Norton.

'I suppose you are insured against such accidents,' the Vicar said as he viewed the scene.

'Oh no, Vicar, but all the damage my men have done will be paid for by me, and the gravestones replaced. It won't cost a fortune.'

Janet kept her word but the chapter of accidents continued. One of the men lost a couple of fingers on the circular saw. Janet paid his wages while he recovered and gave him compensation. But Janet was in business and on the whole it was successful. With Taffy at her beck and call, loads of logs were delivered to the village and beyond, keeping the Welshman and his woodmen employed in the winter. The circular saw sang its tune in Janet Maxwell's brookside meadow.

Janet's stay at the commune had convinced her that 'Free Love' was the way of life for her. One thing to her credit was that she was no threat to the married men of Ayshon, but bachelors, widowers, and ex-husbands were welcome at Ivy Cottage. What became of this American lady? She just faded away, the cottage sold, the lorry and saw-bench no more. The last sight of Janet Maxwell was as she was driven away from the village by Taffy the Welshman in a very smart car.

CHAPTER ELEVEN

CRICKET WITH THE MAJOR

During the war the old cricket ground had been under the plough, growing wheat and barley for the war effort. When Major Sanderson arrived, a Social Centre Committee had purchased another field to be used as a sports ground. Typical of the Worcestershire land, Plovers Piece was 5 acres of undulating pasture. Ridge and furrow indicated that strip cultivation had been used before the Inclosure of 1783. It was not an easy field to form into a cricket ground.

The Major, who became chairman of the Social Centre, sent Phil Grafton with his large Crawler tractor to level the field. His cultivator made a start by drawing the tops of the ridges into the furrows. The Major's bill for the work, received by the Treasurer, was stamped PAID. He was like that, a village benefactor. Few knew of the Major's generosity; those of us who did were grateful.

Many folk remembered the old cricket ground, lovingly tended by the chap from the post office. It was a pitch envied by cricketers from far and wide. Plovers Piece was a problem, and filling in the furrows upset the drainage. Tales of Stocky, the umpire, who gave players out LBW when he wanted his tea, and of Archie, who hit a ball to Gloucester 20 miles away (it landed in a railway truck), were still remembered by a few of us. A contractor was engaged to level Plovers Piece and prepare the cricket pitch and the grass was sown in September.

What about a pavilion the Committee questioned, but the Major knew of a suitable shed high on the Cotswolds which could be made into a shelter and a place to keep the gear. A member brought it to the field and it served its purpose.

Fixtures arranged for May had to be played away because of the bad drainage of the ground. Despite the Major's farming problems cricket kept him happy. He had played for one of the Home Counties and was a first-class batsman. No one made big scores at Plovers Piece, as the wickets were unpredictable, but the Major did score 104 one Saturday.

So those first few years of peace brought the very English game back to the village. LBW decisions by our umpire were not of Dickie Bird's standard. In fact, it was inadvisable even to let the ball hit the pads or the finger went up from the bowler's end.

Selection committees at Hawthorn Farm on Monday nights are memorable. On one occasion two of our best bowlers were unable to play the following Saturday and a sense of gloom fell over the six of us in the Major's lounge as we sat on the fine antique chairs.

'Do we play to win or is it a game?' the Chairman and captain asked. 'For me it's a game. Some of you want to cancel the match I know. Harrington are anxious to come. I propose the fixture remains, although unfortunately I can't be in the team due to an important appointment.'

By a majority decision the fixture was cancelled, and the Secretary wrote to the visitors. Next day, in the fruit market at Evesholme, the captain of the visitors, a market gardener, said to me, 'Can't you muster a team for Saturday? We look forward to coming to Ayshon.'

Pondering over the Selection Committee's discussion it struck me that I could form a team without the two fast bowlers. Around the village eleven men were found, and so the visitors came. As captain, I put Roy, my tractor driver, and John, who worked in industry, to open the bowling. Wickets fell to the bowlers and the visitors were all out for 62. Over tea we all sensed victory, but down came the rain and no one will ever know whether we would have won or otherwise.

Away matches were fun. Few of the players had cars so we loaded up the pre-war Austin 12s, the Ford Anglias, taking the representatives of Ayshon to the Cotswolds and the Vale. One memorable match had us struggling at Stanway, where the ground is picturesque, surrounded by copper beech trees, and the pavilion has a fabulous thatched roof. The Stanway opening batsmen were scoring freely despite our fast bowlers. The Major, a genius for experimenting, tossed the ball to me. 'You have a couple of overs,' he said with his usual broad smile. He knew that I was a reasonable bat at number 5 but not a bowler.

The second ball of my first over sent the middle wicket flying past the keeper and Stanway's opening batsman was out. Oh, the inquest as the Major, laughing and congratulating me and the rest of the team, scrutinised the wicket.

'It's that plantain the ball pitched on,' our wicket keeper said to the Major as the next batsman came to the crease.

'Keep the ball on that length,' our captain said with a smile. 'That was a good ball.' Or was it a bad stroke, I wondered.

In my two overs no more wickets fell and I went back to Fine Leg. Whether we won that day doesn't really matter. It was as the Major said as we were homeward bound: 'What a good game, a pleasant field and tea under the thatch of the pavilion.'

To play cricket after the end of the war was a bonus. Village cricket was amateur, enjoyable, and sometimes very funny.

Playing at a village around the Hill the Major and I were batting at a field adjoining the Avon River. It was getting late, towards 7 o'clock, time to end the match. We were running singles until

breathless. The Major remarked that, for one over, my bat was immovable in front of the stumps. He was laughing his head off. To be at the other end with such a batsman as Frank Sanderson was a privilege. One single after another brought our score very close to the home team's.

'It's 7 o'clock' calls came from the pavilion. We played on and won a little after seven!

Wickets were pretty rough as a rule in those days. Another match saw us enter a field where a herd of Hereford cows and their calves had left cow-pats on the out field. A very rough wicket had been fenced with barbed wire; it was a challenge to our team. Our first four batsmen, with their copybook stance, straight bat in front of the middle wicket, didn't last long. Some were caught behind, one LBW. Batting with Phil Grafton's son, we had a case conference in mid-wicket, deciding to take guard on leg stump, and stand away on the leg side, as the ball was going anywhere but at the wicket. This way with cross bats we made a few runs, the fielders gathering the ball from among the cow-pats. Their wives or mothers no doubt had to wash those white flannels by hand in those days before the washing-machine.

Our captain, Major Frank Sanderson, a rare breed of gentleman, laid the foundations of what is today a cricket team of high standard in Ayshon.

CHAPTER TWELVE

THE RAMS AND THE LEGIONERS

The Major's projects at Hawthorn Farm had so often been disappointing. The outdoor pigs in The Roughs, lambing losses, etc. Of the mixed lot of sheep on the hill it was often hard to know which ones belonged to the Major and which were claimed by Harry Lock. Above The Roughs the thistles grew like trees. Phil Grafton mowed them down with his great Crawler tractor, pulling a trailer mowing-machine. The result was a great deal more tidy, but the left-over stems of the plants were a hazard for the grazing sheep. Scabs around the mouths of the lambs were diagnosed as orf by the local Vet. The purple dye of the gentian violet used for treatment gave the lambs colour around their mouths like that of tinted hair at a hairdressing salon. The lambs recovered but were not in good condition, not a good flock for the market.

I never knew why but the Major cleared the farm of the mixed sheep and bought in a pedigree flock of Kerry Hill ewes to mate with Kerry Hill rams and to breed rams for sale. To begin with, he put the flock in the doubtful hands of Harry Lock, who had let him down so often.

The flock of ewes were turned out with the rams into a field known as Ten Acre Piece and never have I seen such an even and good-looking lot of sheep come from the Welsh border. They should have thrived on this farm where the climate is milder than their home country. Old farmers always said 'Never take sheep north of their native land.' The Kerrys were coming somewhat south and to where the winters are less severe.

It was September, the grass was plentiful, the outlook for some good lambs seemed promising. However, autumn fogs and frosts created a shortage of keep, and the ewes, now in lamb, lost condition. Harry Lock should have known that the flock needed plenty of feed rich in protein and that the kale up the lane should be fed ad lib with sweet clover hay. But the ewes went short and the lambing began soon after Christmas. Harry Lock kept the best of the ram lambs to sell for what the Major hoped to be good prices at the autumn sales. The rest were castrated. It was a sad sight that summer to see the potential ram lambs, half the size they should have been, suckling from their half-starved mothers.

The September ram sales were in full swing. The Major entered ten of the Kerry Hills for the Builth Wells Sale. He and Harry Lock loaded them onto his pick-up truck early that September morning, and the Major and his shepherd set out on their 70-mile trek to Wales.

On arrival at the sale the Major looked somewhat aghast at the other rams to be auctioned. Never had he seen such a trim lot of sheep. They were clipped flat across their backs giving them width; no hairdresser could have trimmed them to such a nicety. Frank Sanderson walked back to his pick-up truck where his ten rams were, to put it mildly, very plain, immature and stunted.

Harry Lock said, 'Where do we unload them, Major?'

The answer came without hesitation: 'They will be unloaded back at Hawthorn Farm. You have made a fool of me, Harry. I'm not unloading this lot to be made a laughing stock.' Harry Lock waited, but worse was to come.

'It's like this, Harry. When we get home you will have your cards. This is the last time I've been tricked by you.'

The two men in the pick-up turned towards home; ten rams were unloaded and joined the rest of the flock.

In the end the Major did manage to sell the sheep. One day a man loading my wheat onto his lorry asked, 'Do you know anyone who has sheep for sale?' His words set me thinking.

'I know where some rams are – not very good 'uns – up at the Major's farm.'

Geoff went and viewed the flock and bought them at £2 10s each.

Back at his Cotswold holding, he castrated the year-old rams, got them fat, and sold them as clean wethers at market.

As a neighbour Major Sanderson was second to none, and it hurt me to see him exploited by Harry Lock and, to a lesser extent, by Phil Grafton. No farmer could have survived with such employees. In a field adjoining my farm we saw his men knock off work every day at 12.30 and they never did a stroke until 2.30. There they sat by a fire on the Hill, taking two hours for dinner instead of one. My men were disgusted by this. One young chap climbed over the fence after the men had gone home soon after four – they should have worked till five – he left a note for them to read the next day. In large letters he wrote: DON'T SPEND SO MUCH TIME AROUND THIS FIRE. The Major's men never knew who wrote the note. My men kept reasonable time so they were pretty livid at the way the Major was being robbed.

The Major was appreciated for his work for the British Legion and had a special fondness for the ex-servicemen of the First World War. A special service was arranged at the church for the Legion. Folk with cars fetched men from the surrounding villages. After the service that Sunday night the Major entertained the old soldiers at the Old Inn.

The cars of the churchwardens, the Vicar, and Patience Byrd waited to take the men home after an evening sampling the local beer. Grudgingly the car owners took these ex-service men back to their villages.

What a stir that caused – boozing late on the Sabbath, as one churchwarden remarked. But the Major was ready with an answer: 'I suppose it's all right for you, the Vicar, and what are called the Toffs, to spend mornings at cocktail parties?'

CHAPTER THIRTEEN

NEW FACES AT
HAWTHORN FARM

It was a sad day for the village when the Major left, a disillusioned man, selling his lovely Georgian house and the farm to go into semi-retirement at a pig and poultry farm where he looked after the stock. No doubt he missed his cricket; we missed him enormously.

Lynda Sanderson transferred her membership of the Women's Branch of the British Legion to another Worcestershire village and no doubt she became a leading light with the Conservative Party. In fact, the last time we met her she took the chair at one of their rallies. She still had her long cigarette holder. It, like Churchill's cigar, gave her a label.

The Major and his wife have both departed now, but every time I pass that farm and I see that window by the front door porch something stirs inside me, and I remember the days of the Cricket Selection Committee, that mahogany table and those antique chairs where we sat and picked the team. I remember too the days when the War Ag was put in its place by Lynda as she objected to its decision to make Hawthorn Farm Grade 'B'. Lynda had style, and had she been the farmer instead of the Major things might have been different. Harry Lock and Phil Grafton certainly would not have reigned so long.

When Frank Sanderson left Hawthorn Farm the majority of the land was annexed by a neighbouring farmer. This left a few acres with the house and farm buildings. Here Brian Campbell came with his young wife. He had come to the Midlands from a Scottish croft. The 30 acres of hill land was adequate for his small flock of Cheviot

sheep. But Brian was interested in turning the group of farm buildings into an intensive pig farm with the help of Ted Green and Phil Grafton. George Burford was now a pensioner but became a part-time shepherd.

Brian was an enterprising man who had served in the Army doing National Service in the Highland Division. All the new methods of producing pigs from his herd of Landrace sows were employed in the old buildings, now converted, of Hawthorn Farm. Early weaning of the stores and creep feeding did produce many more weaners than the traditional two litters a year. Every few days a tanker brought its load of skim milk from the creamery 10 miles away. The weaners were fed on products of the day plus barley meal with supplements, and soon made the weight and the sort of bacon the housewife demanded in those post-war years.

It was evident that Brian Campbell was making an impact on Hawthorn Farm and the village of Ayshon, farming in a way that had never been practised before. Old George Burford, who tended the grass-land flock of ewes on the Hill, had seen it all, following the plough in his youth and hand-milking when the farm had been run by a Frank Peart before the First World War. He was dubious of Brian's practices in the piggeries. In the pub he went on about modern ways of farming to Ted Green, and how the family pig had

had its bristles burnt with straw before it was cut into flitches. Mr and Mrs Campbell just smiled at George's logic, as he called it.

'It's not natural, lad, for pigs to have more than two litters a year, that's nature. You know, when the young pigs are weaned early and fed on crumbs as they call it, the sows come on brimming [on heat] directly and are ready for the boar. They'll produce many more than two litters a year – but it's not natural.'

Landrace pigs do make the sides of bacon needed today. George said that just as they were about to put on weight they went to the slaughterhouse. (George remembered the time when pigs were killed for bacon at 20 score pounds, and the bacon, my, it was good, he said, with enough fat left in the pan to fry the eggs and fried bread.) But that was not his problem; he was, as he stated, a part-time shepherd.

Ted Green fed the pigs while Phil Grafton hauled the slurry from the pens up to the pasture on the Hill. The limestone hill had never had such treatment. Where the grass had been sparse, George's ewes now thrived on wild white clover, pasture nurtured by pig manure. 'Your sheep wouldn't look so kind on the Hill if the grass was not fertilised by the pig slurry,' Ted told him often.

'It's all changed, Gaffer,' George said one morning as master and man sorted some fat lambs for market. 'No disrespect, Mr Campbell, for you produce what the housewife wants I suppose. Now these lambs, it's true they be plump and no doubt tender but not much weight. Now when Frank Peart farmed this land and kept Cotswold and Oxford ewes on turnips, the tegs and wethers sold at more than a year old were as big as donkeys. They looked over the hurdles at the shepherd. They made joints of mutton to be sure.'

Every Friday when Brian's three men finished their work they were paid in the kitchen where Molly Campbell had installed an Aga cooker. Like so many of the housewives from over the border Mrs Campbell loved cooking. As George Burford said when he, Ted and Phil were given a slice of her cake with a cup of tea on those pay-days. ''Tis somewhat different from boughten cake.'

The Campbells had their evening meal at 7 o'clock and were able to sit with George and Ted for a while over a cup of tea. Phil

Grafton went home to his wife, Mary. On those Friday evenings the Campbell's dinner was cooking ready for 7 o'clock, and George and Ted were loath to leave the warmth of the kitchen.

George was forever reminiscing about Frank Peart's farming. 'You remember him, Ted?' he would say. 'But you be a bit younger than me. Oh, he were twenty stone if he were a pound. He used to ride in his float beside the wagons when the men were pitching the hay. If they didn't move fast enough along between the walleys he'd shout "hold tight" to the man on the load. Alf and Jim Badger pitched the hay, Ted led the two horses pulling the wagon. It was all go in those days.' His mouth full with another slice of Molly's cake, he added, 'Sixteen bob a week the Badgers had, while my wages were six shillings.'

Being new to the village, the Campbells enjoyed George and Ted's tales of Hawthorn Farm before the First World War. 'Alf Badger was a farm shepherd, but I won't tell you Ma'am, about some of his practices, not just before you have your dinner. Good night to you both. But before I go, it's around the village that there are folk complaining of the smell from the piggery. No names, Master Campbell, but the one chap who's come here recently and pokes the swallows' nests from under the eaves of his house is the muck stirrer.'

Brian and Molly were worried about George's last bit of news and wondered how anyone in a village could complain about the smell of pigs. . . .

George knew that there was a different attitude to country ways and farming since the Major had left. The days of Frank Peart's occupation of Hawthorn Farm had been so different. Frank had been a law unto himself. The interference of those whom George called the 'Townees' had started, village life was going to change. There was a feeling that the village was now just a dormitory for the folk who worked and shopped in Town. Children bussed away to school in Town lost the benefits of country life. They left at 8 o'clock, returning at 5 as their parents joined the traffic jams in their cars. But George and Ted's stories at the Old Inn were classic and folk came in their cars from the neighbouring towns to hear of times past. Ted told of a family, Holt by name, who planted nasturtiums outside the front gate of their cottage. A flock of sheep driven past with their lambs just ate the whole lot, flowers, leaves and all. 'Salad days,' one chap said with a chuckle.

'You see,' Ted commented, 'I was sorry to see it happen but the roadside verge is not the place to plant nasturtiums. It's the same now with the milking cows. They like to walk on the grass as they go from the field to the milking parlour. The tarmac is hard on their feet. Well, the chap who got rid of the swallows, he kept the grass cut in front of his house. The cows as they had done for years took the easy route!'

'I know,' George added. 'When the bree flies be busy in July Master Brown's cows run like the Devil under Holt's drooping ash tree to ward off those flies. I fancy Master Holt and Farmer Brown ain't exactly first cousins.'

Meanwhile, the story of the smell outside Hawthorn Farm had wafted to the Parish Council and the District Council. Brian was not making a fortune with his pigs, employing just two men with George as part-time shepherd. He and Molly looked around the eighteenth-century farm buildings, a stone barn which housed some of his sows, a cart-horse stable converted for fattening pigs, a long shed where Frank Peart had kept his wagon, and further on a nineteenth-century nag stable converted into a piggery. He had spent a mint on the modernisation of those buildings for his use. If this was the attitude of folk today why worry working seven days a week just to produce bacon.

A friend he met at The Club in Evesholme told him, 'You're sitting on a gold mine.' He knew for a fact there were very few building sites available in Ayshon and that selling the land, the barn, the stables, etc., to a developer was a distinct possibility.

Eventually, plans were passed for a number of dwellings and all of the farm buildings were sold to a developer. 'They beunt a gwain to convert those historic old buildings into houses?' George Burford asked Brian.

'Well, George,' Brian replied, 'I'll keep you on with the sheep on the Hill, but I'm afraid Ted and Phil will have to find other work.

The breeding sows are going. I'm having a sale together with the equipment, and, between me and you, perhaps the organisers of the complaints about the smell have done me a good turn. The buildings for houses were worth more than I thought.'

George mopped his brow, then lit his pipe, saying, 'I be mortally sad 'cause I don't know what Master Peart would have thought. How many houses be planned, Sir?'

'There will be about ten dwellings, including a terrace of bungalows in what you called the cowshed.'

Ted found a job working for a lady in the next village who ran a riding school. After the finalisation of the sale Brian and Molly found that they could afford to employ Phil in the garden and orchard, where he replanted some of the old fruit trees. When Brian was questioned about the barn conversions he mused for a while over his drink at The Club, then came out with, 'It's urbanisation of the village. It's happening almost everywhere. The community no longer exists. Money, along with the motor car, has now replaced even God. So few folk walk the lanes any more. Folks come to the village inn in their sports cars, drinking gin and tonic and eating scampi and chips.'

So Brian and Molly settled down to a semi-retirement but time dragged, and after a year living on their investments they decided to return to their native Scotland. Their croft near Oban was not for them this time, but they bought a property in the Border country where they could retain their little flock of Cheviot ewes and live in relative peace away from the strains and stresses of so-called village life.

The advertisement of the sale of Hawthorn Farm with buildings and 7 acres of land in *The Sunday Times* caught the eye of a stockbroker's wife from Wimbledon. Pamela Bainbridge had a yen for her and her husband, Lionel, to buy a property on the Worcestershire/Gloucestershire border. One reason was that their daughter, Heather, was now studying at Cheltenham Ladies College. Although Heather was only sixteen, Lionel had dreams of her one day marrying a young merchant banker.

One weekend when Heather was home from college, Pamela took her an early morning cup of tea. 'What's that yellow magazine you are reading, dear?'

Heather retorted, 'Oh, that's the *Farmers Weekly*. I take it every week.'

'Not quite the sort of thing you should be reading,' her mother suggested.

'But Mummy, we all originate from the land. It's basic in all of us to get back to the simple life.'

'And the book on the table?'

'Oh, that's *The Gentleman of the Party*. It's terrific writing by A.G. Street.'

'You're at an age between a child and an adult. I don't blame you for your ideas; but it will pass.'

Heather spent a lot of her time away from the college with her friend Fiona Williams, whose father farmed near Tewkesbury. She and Fiona helped with the milking.

'Oh, Daddy, they have a beautiful Hereford bull called Samson. We feed him and muck him out. He's so friendly.'

'Don't talk to me about friendly bulls, girl. I've seen bullfights in Spain. I'd like to know what you intend to do with your life.'

'Oh, I'd love to go to Cirencester Agricultural College and study farming.'

Lionel, who had smoked one cigar after another by the fireside, replied, 'There's no money in farming except when there's a war on.'

The Farming Programme came on television and Heather turned the sound up. Lionel cried out almost in despair, 'For God's sake, turn the sound down if you must watch it. I come in here to the sound of cows bawling, and the sight of some chap up to his backside in muck telling some television reporter about his milk yield. Farmers cost the tax payer millions of pounds producing food no one wants.'

The Bainbridges went to view Hawthorn Farm. A little old man, bent with age, in dusty corduroy trousers, was repairing a stone wall at the end of the orchard. He doffed his cloth cap respectfully. 'Sir, are you interested in this old house? I live in the cottage and if you buy, you'll be my landlord. I've been here, man and boy, for over sixty years. I've been looking after the place since the Master Campbell left. My name is George Burford.'

Lionel looked at his work on the wall and asked him if he was prepared to work for him if he did buy the farm. George agreed, saying, 'I'll have a go, but I'm not as young as I used to be.'

The next day, back in Wimbledon, Lionel took time off from the office. Having decided to buy Hawthorn Farm he was making plans for his future. 'It's like this, Pamela. When we get to Ayshon I'm only going in three days a week at the most. Young Austin, he's dependable. But what can we do to get Heather to stay with us and keep her away from those Williamses? It's a problem.'

Pamela, as ever diplomatic when Lionel was making plans, replied, 'Buy her a pony. It can graze in the orchard.'

'Oh, you know what she said about the "Head Scarf and Pony Club Brigade", but it is worth thinking about. She has ridden on the Common.'

One evening after dinner at their Wimbledon home, Lionel said, 'I wonder what that girl's up to back at Cheltenham. I'll ring her at college.'

'Should you, Lionel? Is it wise?'

'Hello. Is that the Principal? Could I have a word with our daughter, Heather Bainbridge? It's her father speaking.'

The answer shocked Lionel. He thought at least she would be studying. 'Sorry, Mr Bainbridge. Heather has gone to Mr Gwyn Williams's farm with Fiona and is staying overnight.'

As he put the phone down Lionel said, 'Get me a drink, Pamela. You can ring those Williams folk. I might say too much. My God! The first opportunity and that girl is in the cow yard.' So Pamela phoned the farm.

'Nesta Williams speaking. Yes, Heather is here. Would you like to speak to her? She is out in the yard helping my husband and Fiona to calve a heifer.'

It was a difficult calving. The young Friesian had been served by a

Hereford bull and the calf's head was finding it hard to see the light of day.

'Hold the heifer's head you two girls, while George and I try to calve her.'

'Isn't it wonderful!' Heather cried as the nose of the calf appeared between its front legs. As it fell to the straw, black with a white face, Heather and Fiona loosed the chain from its mother's neck and it licked the newborn calf.

'Mummy,' Heather had come to the phone and spoke like some midwife. 'We have calved a heifer without sending for the Vet. It's a beauty. Now it's on its feet sucking its mother. I feel so happy. How are you and Daddy?'

Pamela spoke abruptly. 'Daddy's annoyed that you have wasted no time in becoming a country bumpkin. He says it's so unladylike. Can I speak to Mrs Williams?'

Mrs Williams came back to the phone. 'Yes Mrs Bainbridge, I'll see that she has a bath before going to bed. I'll look after her. We must meet some day.'

'Yes, I'll look forward to that when we move into Hawthorn Farm.'

In Fiona's bedroom, Heather was still awake at 11 o'clock. The calving of the heifer, her first experience with such an event, was still foremost in her mind. She said to Fiona that sometimes nature can be cruel when animals suffer.

'Oh, Daddy does give injections when his cows are in pain, but the worst thing to happen is when a cow has a breach birth and the calf comes backwards. The hair is stroked the wrong way and it's often dry. That means a visit from the Vet.'

The girls talked some more about the animals, and about themselves and their plans for the future. They talked about boys, and who they would marry. 'I wouldn't unless I loved him . . . and he would have to be a farmer,' Heather had her ideals.

The Bainbridges had decided to convert one wing of the house into a flat for a chauffeur and housekeeper, and put an advert in a

Cheltenham paper. Phil Grafton and his wife, Mary, who had been living in a council house in the village, got the positions, and the flat was soon ready for their occupation. They moved in at Michaelmas; the Bainbridges delayed their own move for a fortnight.

Old George Burford was to work in the fruit and vegetable garden while Phil Grafton planned the lawns and borders, the shrubbery and the orchard. Phil, away from tractor driving, found his bent in the garden and orchard. He could graft fruit trees, and kept bees. He was more of a fancy gardener than ever he was a farm worker with his tractor. And he was a mine of information about the village.

CHAPTER FOURTEEN

Two Types of Farming

After the Major left Hawthorn Farm and Brian Campbell just retired, leaving the farm, the farm buildings, and a few acres on the Hill, it is interesting to learn what happened to the other 200-odd acres.

The man who annexed the land was Tom Holder, a very progressive farmer, whose property in the adjacent village joined Hawthorn Farm. Tom was an organic farmer some years before the words were in common use. He kept a herd of Hereford cattle and a flock of pedigree Suffolk sheep, and farmed the land in rotation. His land under and on the slopes of the Hill became a haven for birds, beasts and wild flowers. Tom was up to date in cultivation but farmed without chemicals. His woodlands, mostly spinneys, were a natural sanctuary for badgers and foxes, and the large swaths of land left on headlands rang with the song of peewits and larks.

Sheep hitched, or folded, on turnips and swedes had long since become uneconomic, as had the growing of mangolds; these practices were just too labour intensive. Tom grew acres of kale where the Suffolk sheep were enclosed in pens by electric fences, a practice which put fertility into his land and was easily managed.

His neighbours' chemically grown crop of wheat resulted in boasts of 3 tons plus per acre, but Tom's land increased in fertility in three ways. First of all, from the use of manure from corn-fed sheep; secondly, from the ploughing in of green manure, clover aftermath, mustard, etc.; and thirdly, from his insistence on fallowing the land in rotation. So Tom's corn crops compared favourably with his neighbours and were free from chemicals. In addition to the swaths of uncultivated headlands he left some fields with long stubble through the winter to encourage partridges. There was a sweetness in his hay bales, which consisted not of rye grass but of a mixture of clovers that smelt as sweet as honey in late June.

Here was a farm visited by many who wanted to learn how the land could be worked without chemicals. One hears of tenancy agreements of years ago which forbade the tenant to sell hay or straw from the farm. Everything was eaten by stock or turned into manure. Tom Holder practised in like manner in those years after the war, and strangely the good heart of the soil and his careful management kept his crops virtually free from blight and disease.

Tom Holder kept his buildings in such a splendid state they were, in some ways, superior to some cottages in the village. Even the ruin of some ancient chapel stood as a memorial to the care of Tom Holder. What Tom did on his farm was often quoted on the BBC. Here was food for thought for the young farmers, methods practised for generations on many farms in the vales and hills on the Worcestershire/Gloucestershire border.

Here, farmers who worked land without livestock were happy to rent out fields to market gardeners, for one year, for sprout growing. The Vale growers who rented hill land were able to grow sprouts more easily after myxomatosis had killed 94 per cent of rabbits in 1954. The sprouts, planted on the square 3 feet apart, had previously been kept clear of weeds by the horse-hoe. The tractors with hydraulic lifts and power take-off now cropped the young sprouts planted both ways, leaving little for the men to hoe around the plants. Maybe the life of the sprout-grower was simplified by the myxomatosis and the row-crop tractor. It often resulted in gluts of vegetables and low market prices.

One problem with sprout growing in a hot dry summer is aphids or white blight. So many chemicals have been tried, from Bellamite to Nicotine dust, but the blight multiplies under the leaves. In those years, scientists developed a systemic spray of a metastatic compound, a systemic insecticide, which when sprayed on the plants gave a 100 per cent kill of blight. Oh, the directions were that the sprouts were not to be marketed for so many weeks after the application. No one knew at the time the effect it would have on wild birds when the spray lay in little puddles on the sprout leaves on hot summer days. Larks, peewits, finches, all drank of that lethal liquid and were killed in hundreds on the fields. After a few weeks, the sprouts were clean of blight, a bonus to the grower, but death to wild birds.

George Burford remembered the corn crakes, or land railes he called them, and other birds which have become either rare or extinct because of modern farming.

'I recall old Frank who farmed yer when I was what was known as a Hobbledehoy, a teenager I suppose today, neither a man nor a boy. Well, I know the man's dead and gone but it was criminal what he did. You see, he had a crop of peas high on the hill and the rooks, jackdaws and pigeons were playing merry hell with the peas that were almost fit to pick. Frank went up there with his horse and trap. He was a big man mind, wouldn't have been able to walk that steep cart track. He took with him a sack of wheat which he had dressed with strychnine, terribly poisonous chemical. He broadcast the wheat around the headlands of the pea field to poison the crows. Next day, he sent me and Ted Green up the hill with a spade to bury the dead birds. It was a right mess to be sure. There were crows, pigeons, larks, peewits, partridges, stone dead in the pea rows. It took me and Ted some time to bury them, and that was not all. Some of the rooks made for the rookery at the next village and dropped dead in the road in front of the police station. The gamekeeper there came and warned Old Frank, but 'twas a dangerous thing.'

CHAPTER FIFTEEN

THE MOVE

On his first train journey back into London after the move to Hawthorn Farm, Lionel looked at the countryside as he travelled through it and noticed that, beyond Oxford, it looked groomed, the harvest was in, occasionally a tractor was ploughing the stubble. To Lionel, the land looked unoccupied, field after field devoid of workers. Who does all the harvesting and ploughing? A herd of Friesian cows were on their way from the milking parlour to their pastures. One man followed maybe 150 animals.

Lionel's mind wandered once more. 'One hundred and fifty cows, they are worth some money. . . . Farmers, I'm sure that's one, are self-employed. Where are the old agricultural labourers?'

At Paddington one of Lionel's clerks met him at the station to take him to his office.

Pamela had Mary Grafton working in the house, a pleasant country woman, the daughter of a Bredon Hill shepherd. She was a good cook and as housekeeper she engaged Maud to do the cleaning and washing.

'Oh, good morning, Ma'am. Welcome to your new home and to Ayshon.' These words came from a rather breathless George Burford, who had arrived with an enormous barrow load of garden produce – potatoes, runner beans, tomatoes, plums, apples, etc. – for Mary Grafton to stock the kitchen.

'George, you mustn't overdo it. What a load!'

George replied, 'Well Ma'am, it's Michaelmas, a time of plenty. You know the old saying "Michaelmas, or a little before, half the apple is thrown away with the core, Christmas, or a little bit after, if it's as sour as a crab it's Thank you Master." These apples won't keep long but when I pick the keepers, Bramleys mostly, there's room in the loft.'

'Thank you, George. I notice you have finished the boundary wall.'

'Yes, Ma'am. I heard a whisper that the Master might be getting a pony for Miss Heather. I'm mending fences and there's a shed at the top of the orchard that would make a stable by the water trough.'

'You take it gently, George, we need you here for a long time.' As George was about to leave after unloading his barrow the phone rang. It was the Vicar, inviting the family to tea that afternoon. Pamela then rang Heather at college to tell her of the invitation.

'Sorry, Mummy. It's Young Farmers' Club tonight. I'm going with Fiona. It's a group meeting, terribly important. A man from the Ministry of Agriculture is the speaker. We are so lucky to get him. He's going to talk about alternative crops to cereal: comfrey, linseed, sunflowers, etc. He says there is a market waiting for goats' milk, it's so healthy. The Farmers' Union and the Agricultural Workers' Union have delegates involved. Everyone is so concerned with the food mountains.'

'Heather . . .'

'Yes, Mummy?'

'Unions smack of Communism. Something your grandfather fought against in the war. You would throw away all that our ancestors gave, and get rid of royalty. I'm shocked that you mix with such reactionaries.'

'Oh, Mummy! You're a hundred years behind the times. What would the workers in the motor industry do without the unions and shop stewards to represent the workers?'

'Oh, I give up!' Pamela sighed as she put the phone down.

Life was not easy for Lionel. Heather was a permanent problem. Then Mavis Bennet, Pamela's mother, rang on the Thursday afternoon. 'Could we come down for the weekend? We are longing to see your country house.'

Pamela replied resignedly, 'Of course you may.' But she suspected that Lionel would not be happy that they were coming so soon after the move.

When Pamela's parents, Claud and Mavis Bennet, arrived Mavis asked if Heather was home. Lionel replied, 'No, she's not here. She's at Gwyn Williams's farm with her friend Fiona calving cows, mucking out the bull, up to her knees in shit.'

'Oh, darling, don't use that word.'

'Well, that describes it.'

'This chap Williams is supposed to be a progressive farmer, got the idea from Professor Boutflour who milked the cows three times a day. He went to Cirencester.'

Then Claud, Pamela's father, got a word in at last. 'Lionel, he's not a country bumpkin; he is educated, in a way.' The conversation then took the usual turn to feather-bedded farmers.

'What is the world coming to?' Mavis said loudly and poor Lionel's head was throbbing. 'These farmers are cruel. Battery hens, sweat boxes for pigs, and those putrid sprays that kill the birds. I'm old enough to remember when farmers in cord trousers with their rosy faces cared for the land *and* its animals.'

'Oh, I'm with you, Mother, in a lot of what you say, but when cows stood knee-deep in ponds and spread TB, young chaps and girls went down in their thousands with what was called consumption, TB of course.'

CHAPTER SIXTEEN

THE RUNT IN THE LITTER

Lionel had a lie-in on the Saturday morning. He was wondering what exactly he was exposing himself to, this so-called peaceful country life, with no street lighting, and far from the theatre. He knew little of hunting and fishing, and didn't really want to, and what of village cricket, church, garden parties? 'What have I let myself in for?' he thought. 'Pamela has adapted – she would!' (She was a socialiser who loved to show off her clothes and social standing.)

Heather was coming for the weekend. Phil was to fetch her from the Williams's farm in Pamela's Volvo. 'Get her back here promptly, Phil. We expect her for lunch.' These words had sent the chauffeur/gardener tearing down the drive. 'I'll do my best, Sir,' came the reply.

At Gwyn Williams's farm a sow had just delivered a litter of piglets, farrowing in the loose box next to the cowsheds. (Fiona explained that the farrowing rail between the sow and the litter was to prevent the mother from lying on the new-born piglets.) There were ten piglets in all, Gloucester Old Spots. Gwyn kept half a dozen sows and sold the weaners at eight weeks at Gloucester Market. One piglet was much smaller than the rest, what country folk called a runt. Nine of the litter were suckling the sow but the little runt stood alone in the corner of the loose box. Heather could not take her eyes off that little pig. 'What a shame,' she cried to Fiona. 'It's not getting any milk.'

At that moment the Williams's cowman arrived to feed the sow, and said that he was going to kill the runt. 'Some call it a nisgal; they never live.'

'You're not going to kill it?' Heather said angrily. 'It's not fair, give it a chance.'

'We always do,' Fiona remarked. 'It's not worth the trouble.'

'I'll take it home when Phil comes for me.'

The cowman was perplexed at the young girl's spirit but assured her that it would die as sure as God made little apples. When Phil arrived to take Heather home he was worried what Lionel's reaction would be. 'Don't you think your Dad will be vexed, Miss, if you take that little pig to Hawthorn Farm. Come on, I've got to take you home.'

Heather was firm. 'I don't care. That little pig is not going to be killed, and can I have a bottle of milk, Fiona?'

With some trepidation Phil Grafton took Heather and the piglet on the short journey to Hawthorn Farm. Heather wrapped the little animal in a potato sack and held a bottle of milk in one hand as she sat on the back seat of the car nursing the runt.

At Hawthorn Farm Heather carried the little pig to the stable. Phil followed with the bottle of milk. Pamela was waiting to meet her daughter in the stable yard and could not believe her eyes. 'What on earth have you got there, Heather? Oh, my God! It's a little pig, and your clothes! You positively stink. You can't keep that pig here. I'll run you back with it to the Williams's farm. How disgusting, and your grandparents are here for the weekend.'

George Burford arrived at that moment with a basket of apples, some James Grieve from the orchard. He was chuckling between puffs at his pipe. 'Oh, you have got a little runt there, Miss, some call them Dillons.'

'Yet another name,' Heather thought.

'What do you think, George?' Pamela said with some acidity.

'Well, we allus knocked them on the head. It will never make a pig. More trouble than they are worth. Oh, it's a Gloucester Old Spot to be sure. Hardy pigs mind, but the bacon rind's as hard as the Devil's back teeth. They be orchard pigs, they used to live on windfall apples and a bit of meal. That's made my day, seeing a Gloucester Old Spot, pity it's a runt. The best of luck with it, Miss Heather, you'll need it!'

Pamela listened carefully to George's words of wisdom, and continued, 'You heard what George says, Heather, we should take it back to the farm. It's not funny, George, it will have to go, Gloucester Old Spot or whatever.'

'I've got a bottle of milk, Mother, and Fiona has given me a teat, one they keep for orphan lambs.'

Pamela stumped back to the house, angry, calling back to George, Phil and Heather, 'I'm leaving it to you. I'll have nothing to do with this charade. I just don't know what my husband will say.'

Phil, a sensitive chap, anxious to please, brought a fruit hamper with some straw in the bottom and placed the piglet in the warm. Heather fixed the teat on the neck of the bottle and offered it to the piglet. It took some persuasion for the little mite to suck the still warm milk through the teat.

'It needs keeping warm,' old George said aside to Phil, who had an idea.

'There's an electric chicken lamp in the stable. We can fix that over the hamper after I've plugged it in, and, Miss Heather, leave the rest of the milk in the bottle in the straw, that will keep lukewarm and you can feed the little fella again after dinner.'

George Burford stood there, puffing his pipe and dressed as he always was in cord trousers with Yorks below his knees and his battered trilby hat hiding the mop of grey hair above his rosy face. He chuckled. 'Mind, I wouldn't like to be in your shoes when the Gaffer knows. You won't be very welcome.'

It was with some pluck that Heather went through the back door into the kitchen and met her mother, who greeted her with, 'You are a disgrace. Look at your jeans. Your father's in the drawing-room with your grandparents. He doesn't know about the pig. Don't come near me. You can catch things from animals. Mary, where are you?'

'I'm dusting the hall, Mrs Bainbridge,' Mary answered.

Pamela shouted, 'Come here quickly. Get this girl her dressing gown, run the bath, and you, Heather, strip off here and now, and Mary, put those jeans and shirt to soak in disinfectant.' Then she had second thoughts. 'No, Mary, put them in the garbage bin. I'll get more for her.'

Heather seemed to have more affinity with Mary and Phil Grafton than with her parents. They were real country folk who appreciated her love of animals. Mary thought Heather an interesting mixture. She would have a go at anything. The Graftons were Non-Conformists, members of the Baptist Chapel. Heather, she didn't conform, had her own ideas and didn't trust the so-called 'Establishment'.

After her bath, in her dressing gown, she said so sweetly to Mary, with the voice of a friend rather than the daughter of the mistress of the house, 'Mary . . . .'.

'Yes, Heather.'

'I'm back at college on Monday, would you feed the little pig for me. I'm calling it Juliet. You will, won't you? You are a dear. It's a beautiful creature, a young female, George calls it a gilt, not a guilty thing, that's me, I suppose. Oh, the milk, Mary. I've asked George to get an extra pint from the milkman. I'll pay him, of course. It will get lukewarm under the chicken lamp. I can feel that Juliet is in safe hands with you, Mary. It's only for a week because I come home for half term next weekend. Fiona says that the little pigs soon learn to drink from a trough and then they can have small nuts called weaner crumbs. Fiona will let me have some of course.'

Mary listened to this college student, who she knew was learning the art and practice of farming livestock from the Williamses, from her study of nature, from listening to tips from the Young Farmers' Club. She seemed so distant from her Wimbledon life, and was intrigued, a young enquirer into a whole new world. Mary whispered, 'Your Dad doesn't know about Juliet, does he?'

'No, Mary. He's with my grandparents in the drawing-room discussing politics not pigs. Ha, ha, not that much difference! You are an absolute darling, Mary, you know Dad and Grandpa are completely out of touch with reality. Don't you agree?'

'Oh, Heather, you know I only work here.'

Heather now cleaned up, went to her room, and played a few records before lunch. The question of the runt pig came up after lunch, and Lionel was really steamed up. 'This is not, nor will I allow it to become, an animal sanctuary. I'm not having ailing, scruffy pigs, or any such animals, dumped here when they should be put down.'

Heather, flushed and angry, said, 'What do you mean Dad, not destroyed!'

'Of course,' came the quick reply. 'And who is going to pay the Vet's bills?'

'It won't cost anything if I need the Vet to Juliet.'

Lionel snapped, 'Juliet my foot.'

Heather then said, 'The People's Dispensary for Sick Animals will care for Juliet. One of their team gave a talk at Young Farmers.'

'What is this Young Farmers' Club? Just a lot of swede gnawers?' asked Lionel.

Heather retorted, 'They're a jolly active lot. Farmers are the backbone of the country. Do you know what happened in Germany after the First War? I'll tell you. When the German mark was worthless the only people who had anything to barter with were the farmers. They were the only ones who had any food.'

Heather's grandmother interrupted, and asked what she wanted to do with her life. Heather replied, 'Something practical in agriculture. A chap I know in the Young Farmers' Club, his father farms 1,000 acres of Cotswold land. Acres of barley, very little stock. But their place isn't my idea of a farm, Grandmother.'

Claud chipped in, 'Make no mistake, these Barley Barons are the ones who make the money, cosseted by the Government, and they export tons of grain to the Continent. They are real businessmen so unlike the small farmers in the south-west, tied to the cow's tail.'

Lionel was surprised at Claud's knowledge of agriculture. At her young age, Heather just wondered why farmers had become so political. Claud continued, 'The corn growers in East Anglia and the Cotswolds, with their massive fields, they have pretty good incomes. They take out loans to equip themselves with modern machinery. Now the dog and stick men in the west must manage with outdated equipment discarded by the Barley Barons.'

Lionel had joined a nearby golf club and was chatting to Wilf, a wise Manchester insurance manager, telling him how someone at the club had gone on slating the farmers, calling them yobs living on subsidies, hunting and shooting, until he almost believed it. Wilf laughed. 'Now look here, Lionel, you and I have lived long enough to know that there are bad eggs in every batch. I find the farmers a pretty shrewd, honest lot around here, hard-working. I speak as I find. You did say, Lionel, that your daughter Heather is spending a lot of her time in the cow and sheep pens of Mr Williams. I know Gwyn Williams and have done quite a bit of insurance with him. He's a hard-working lad, very pleasant. You have got a couple of useful chaps in your gardens. Old George Burford and young Phil Grafton. Mind you, Lionel, Phil's a bit of a Bible thumper, nice chap, but a bit allergic to bad language and drink.'

Lionel, drawn in by Wilf's wit and wisdom, said, 'What do you think of the Rector, and his wife? A bit well read for a place like this, I'd say.'

'I only go to church at Harvest, Easter and Christmas. Suppose you'd call me a backslider. In Manchester, as a boy, it was twice a day on Sundays.'

Lionel made no reply but had made up his mind to support the Rector with his presence, and financially too. It seemed a respectable thing to do.

'Had a nice evening, Lionel? Heather's been on the phone. She's going to the November meeting of the Young Farmers' Club tomorrow. It's a public speaking competition.'

'Sounds okay, Pamela. Better there than being in Williams's cow yard for the evening. Yes, Wilf and I had a splendid time at the Pear Tree, nothing fancy, an old-fashioned pub. I feel better for it. How about you?'

Pamela replied, 'Just a quiet time with Mary Grafton. She's a gem, a bit narrow but such a worker. Phil comes from a very old Ayshon family.'

CHAPTER SEVENTEEN

THE PONY

Lionel would never admit it but the autumn tints on the trees in Ayshon Wood gave him the feeling that God was in his heaven and all was right with the world. The war years, 1939–45, were fading into the distant past. Recreation, travel and the abundance of food made life easier. He had two good men, and Pamela had a super housekeeper, with a woman from the village to do the cleaning. The confirmed 'city gent' recognised the coloured pictures of the countryside, something he had never dreamed of in the neon-lit streets of the city. Talks with old George Burford over a morning cup of cider from the barn were a revelation. To think that a man of so little education knew so much and had such humour.

One morning George came shuffling along from the barn with a string of onions. 'We shall get some rain tonight, Sir.'

Lionel, a regular listener to weather forecasts, replied, 'No mention of rain in last night's forecast.'

George replied, 'I've got no time for the Met. Office. The crows this morning be at break necks, dive bombing, then cider making, going in circles, a good sign of rain. Now, Sir, in the summer in the hay field, that was when we made hay, none of this salvage, sometimes we would get a whirlwind and the hay would go in eddies up into the sky, that meant tempest or thunder. Oh, I know the Met. men calls whirlwinds thermals. . . . I got a thermos flask mind.'

George was very critical of modern life; maybe it was partly his way of appearing more of a knave than a fool. His son was a lorry driver, a heavy goods lorry, described by George as a 'damn great dazel'. 'I went with him to Wales last week with a load o' taters. We got on a road past Tewkesbury called The Spur and we went like the clappers. The thing was, there was no need to bother about vehicles coming the other way, they was on another road altogether. You bin on those roads, Sir?'

'Oh, yes George,' Lionel remarked smiling, keeping back a laugh and thinking, 'That's a tale to tell Wilfred Baker when he's doing a short putt on the green at Donnington golf course.' He said out loud, 'I do look forward to some of your experiences, George. We are thinking about buying a pony for Heather, any comment?'

'Well, Sir,' George replied, 'some horse copers be a crooked lot, be careful.'

Lionel was not the only one to enjoy George's stories. Heather also found a lot of pleasure, and acquired some knowledge, from his anecdotes. Heather and George were having a chat one day while cleaning out the piglet's sty. The conversation got round to the subject of farming and what Heather would like to do in that area.

'George,' she told him, 'the sort of farming I would like to do is like Tom Holder's organic farm, over the village boundary.'

George replied, 'Yes, I know Tom Holder's place. His Hereford cattle be a sight for sore eyes. Damn these foreign beasts as be coming yer. Some farms look more like zoos.'

Heather spent a lot of time just talking to George Burford when she was home, and her mother and father would have to remind her to do her homework.

'I'm hoping to have a pony soon, George, and Dad knows nothing of horses. How easy is it to pick a good one?'

George replied with his usual chuckle, 'A good un? Well, the horse copers be a bent lot mind. 'Tis like buying a second-hand car nowadays. I think he should take a farmer with him, or else he might get his fingers burnt.'

Heather was amused at some of the old man's expressions but soon learnt their meaning. George went on about Frank Peart's carter, Jim Badger. 'Now he was a good man with horses, but you know what they say. 'Tis starting again after a rest that kills horses, and sometimes young horses die so old ones be bound to.'

'What did Jim Badger use when his horses were ill, George, before modern veterinary medicines?'

George quickly answered, 'They depended a lot on linseed oil and turpentine, sometimes they gave whisky and beer to horses which were ailing. Frank Peart bought some whisky for Jim to give to one of his horses and I gather Jim drank the whisky. I'll tell you, Miss Heather, that one of the worst things 'osses get is the gripes, they get bloated. Now one year, when I worked as a boy on Hawthorn Farm, Turpin, a big gelding, got out of The Close into the apple orchard and filled his guts with green apples. Jim and Alf were keeping him moving on a halter and he kept lying down. They gave him linseed oil and turpentine to shift the wind in his guts. Mind you, they are in pain and they will come for you open-mouthed if you are not careful. 'Tis a funny thing, horses when they be in good health do get what you might call the collywobbles all the time. Their stomachs rumble but with Turpin the rumbling had stopped and he couldn't stale.'

'Stale, George, what ever is that?' Heather asked.

'To be polite, Miss, 'tis to pass water. Old Jim was listening with his ear up against Turpin's ribs for the rumble. Alf held Turpin on a halter. We hobbledehoys were making such a rattle near by and Jim couldn't hear whether Turpin's guts were rumbling. Oh, the language Jim used to us, 'twas pretty strong, and we had to leave the men to their treatment of Turpin. They walked him around the yard, then into The Close trying to prevent him lying down. At last, after the usual whistling to encourage him to pass water, he staled and the bloat left him.'

Heather went to do her homework and reminded her father how much she wanted a pony to ride. It was so odd that this schoolgirl, a product of city parents who had lived in a luxury home in London, had such a yen for farming. But as she used to say 'We all originate from the land'. Maybe it was a few generations back in the case of the girl from the city. Heather didn't want to be in the 'Headscarf Brigade', or join the pony trekking, show jumping crowd. She wanted one day to raise a herd of cattle, to keep sheep and pigs, to

feel the clay under her feet and see the birth and maturity of farming, both crops and animals. She realised she could never be such a farmer as Tom Holder, who farmed so beautifully with nothing but organic material.

Lionel and Pamela knew that the Williamses had a New Forest pony for Fiona and that sometimes Heather had ridden it, with Fiona alongside on her dad's hunter. 'I think we should meet those Williamses you know,' Lionel suggested, and suss out what the set-up is at their farm. Heather stays there, they seem a decent family. You give them a ring and ask if we can meet sometime, Pamela.'

Pamela picked up the telephone, dialled the number, and put the suggestion to Mrs Williams. 'Yes, Mrs Bainbridge, do come over to coffee at the farm.' Nesta Williams was full of the fact that Heather was such a good friend of Fiona. 'They are good for each other, Mrs Bainbridge.'

'Oh, for goodness sake, call me Pamela, and you are Nesta, it's so much easier. Of course, it's good for Heather to have a taste of the farming side of life, and she and Fiona are tomboys together. The fact is, Lionel, my husband, and I don't want her to take farming so seriously, as if that's all life has to offer a young lady.'

Nesta Williams thought a while before replying. 'I do see your point, Pamela, but ever since I met your daughter, even the first time, it struck me that she was bent on farming. She seems to have a knack with animals. Sometimes women are so much better with livestock than men. I gather your husband, Lionel, would like a word with Gwyn.'

'Yes, Nesta, we have a few acres of pasture land adjoining Hawthorn Farm and know nothing about farming, but we would like your husband's advice because we are thinking of buying Heather a pony.'

A day or two later Lionel and Pamela went to the Williams's farm for coffee. Nesta called her husband, who offered Lionel cider instead. 'I have some good stuff in the cellar, vintage stuff made from Black Taunton and Fox Whelp apples.'

Pamela stayed in the kitchen with Nesta while the two men went to the cellar. After they had drunk a couple of mugs from one of Gwyn's hogshead barrels they went to the stable where Gwyn showed Lionel Fiona's pony and his hunter.

'You know, Gwyn, I hardly know one end of a horse from the other, but your animals look good to me. If I buy Heather a pony would you be kind enough to go with me to a horse sale and advise me, possibly select one. That would be a load off my mind. I've dealt as a stockbroker in millions of pounds, but frankly to buy a pony frightens the daylights out of me. I hear that horse copers, like second-hand car dealers, can do some awful things and con the unsuspecting purchasers. Car dealers, of course, bodge up old cars, put the mileage back on the clock. Gwyn, you advise me. I'll pay the expenses. Heather is not exactly a beginner. She has ridden at a riding school on Wimbledon Common. What she needs is a reliable animal like the one Fiona has got.'

Gwyn Williams was conscious that Heather's father would be sold a pup, what the trade called 'left-handed ones', and thought that for the sake of the two families he would see that Heather had a pony fit for her. He told Lionel that there was a horse sale at Hereford the following week, and that he would take Lionel there in his Land Rover.

'That's okay, Gwyn, but my chauffeur Phil will take us there in my car. That's no problem. Wednesday you say?'

A shepherd tends the young of his flock.
(Photo: Rural History Centre, University of
Reading; 35/32865)

The village sheep fair at the turn of the century. (Photo: Rural History Centre, University
of Reading; 35/27310)

A steam cultivator manufactured by G.F. Bomford at work in the fields around Evesham, *c.* 1915. (Photo: The Almonry, Evesham)

Farm workers pause for refreshment, Harvington, *c.* 1915. (Photo: The Almonry, Evesham)

Hay baling in Harvington after the First World War. (Photo: The Almonry, Evesham)

An early internal combustion engine – an International Harvester Titan – which ran on paraffin. This was one of the popular American machines imported during the First World War. (Photo: Rural History Centre, University of Reading; 35/30697)

The rabbit trapper after a busy day, *c*. 1950. (Photo: Rural History Centre, University of Reading; 35/8424)

A wheelwright absorbed in his craft, *c*. 1930. (Photo: Rural History Centre, University of Reading; 35/25844)

A farmer and his team work with a ridging plough, preparing the field for planting. (Photo: Rural History Centre, University of Reading; 35/29506)

A pre-war planting scene. These women would have been paid about 4s a day. (Photo: Rural History Centre, University of Reading; 35/13487)

Building a rick, 1939. As the horse stands patiently by, hay is unloaded on to the elevator, which is probably being driven by a small oil engine. (Photo: Rural History Centre, University of Reading; 35/28358)

The threshing machine at work, *c.* 1950. Two land girls are cleaning chaff and straw fragments away from the back of the machine – an unpopular job with the other workers. (Photo: Rural History Centre, University of Reading; 35/8930)

Land girls and farm workers in the Evesham area. (Photo: The Almonry, Evesham)

Land girls get to grips with the farm machinery. (Photo: The Almonry, Evesham)

A traction engine driving a chaff cutter, *c.* 1930. (Photo: Rural History Centre, University of Reading; 35/17273)

Local women gather in a war-time crop of spring onions. With no one else to look after them, the women brought even their youngest children along. (Photo: Rural History Centre, University of Reading; slide 4599)

Gwyn, fond of Heather as Fiona's best friend, said to Lionel, 'Your daughter is such a lovely girl and rides Fiona's pony sometimes. She rides well, has what is called a good seat. She needs a Welsh pony about 14 hands, safe in traffic, sound in wind and limb. Now forget about paying me for advice; it's a pleasure and anything we can do for Heather we will.'

When Pamela rang Heather at college telling her that her father proposed buying her a pony the result was a much improved feeling between the daughter and her dad. Of course, she loved him always but found him out of time with modern society and country life. She was delighted and rang back in the evening and told him that it would be such a good thing to have a pony about the place.

On Wednesday morning the day's programme was discussed by the Bainbridges. Lionel insisted that Phil should drive them to Hereford in Pamela's Volvo.

'What on earth for, Lionel?' Pamela exclaimed. 'Why not in the Rolls?' was her idea.

Lionel, trying to look and sound like a sharp businessman, replied, 'For obvious reasons. If those horse copers see us arrive at the sale in a Rolls they will think we are loaded with money.'

Pamela laughed out loud. 'But aren't you loaded with money?'

'This is a different kind of stock market, Pamela, and you should know Wilf Baker warned me at the pub about the ways of dealers,' replied Lionel.

When the Welsh ponies entered the sale ring they all seemed remarkably cheap to Lionel. He noticed that Gwyn didn't make a bid for any of them. Gwyn asked Lionel and Phil to stay and watch the sale while he had a word with a friend from Wales away from the ring. 'You see, Lionel, they often bring the ones here that are unreliable but keep the best at home and find buyers themselves. If I find a chap who has something special at his farm I'll introduce you to him.'

After a while Gwyn returned to the ring with Bryn Evans from Brecon. After introductions he, Lionel, Bryn and Phil left the ring for the car park, where Bryn explained his position. 'I've sold some ponies here today, but if you require something really reliable my daughter's pony is for sale if someone will give the right price. The Welsh mare is 14½ hands. Now eighteen, my daughter is into show jumping and needs a bigger mount. She has hunted the mare regularly and I can warrant it absolutely reliable. Mind you, it will be considerably more money than the ones of unknown quality at the sale. A lot of the plain ones finish up as butcher's meat.' Bryn, keen to sell the mare, continued, 'Come over to my place, it's not that far.'

At the farm near Brecon, Lionel's eyes and Phil's eyes were almost dazzled by a beautiful liver chestnut mare. 'I'll tell you what, Sir,' Bryn was speaking to Lionel, 'would you like to see my daughter ride her?'

'What do you think, Gwyn?' Lionel was still unsure.

Gwyn looked at the pony's mouth, confirming the animal to be six years old. He ran his hand down its legs to check for side bones, examined its hooves, its eyes. 'I can't fault it,' was his assessment.

Mr Evans's daughter put a saddle and bridle on the mare and trotted around the yard and cantered across the cow ground. Lionel cautiously asked Phil what he thought. Phil told him, 'I can only go by looks, Sir, but she looks a picture.'

'It's just a matter of price, Mr Evans. What are you asking?'

'Well, Sir, I can't be fairer, if you buy her and find her unsuitable I'll take her back. She's not a beginner's ride and Gwyn tells me your daughter is quite good on his daughter's pony. I'm asking £850 and I'll warrant her sound and safe in traffic.'

Lionel replied, 'I'll take it. Will you deliver it on Saturday, my daughter will be home from college then.'

Mr Evans said, 'Give me your hand, Sir.'

Lionel held out his hand and Bryn Evans hit it with his open palm, shouting 'Sold.' Lionel gave him a cheque for £850 and Bryn gave him two £5 notes. Lionel was a bit taken aback. 'What's that for, Mr Evans?' he wondered.

'That's Luck Money, Sir. We always give back money when we sell a horse.'

'I'm slowly learning the strange customs of the countryside,' Lionel said to Gwyn. 'Luck Money,' he thought to himself; 'My God! We don't do that in the City. Some of these chaps are really human.'

Phil Grafton fetched Heather home from college on Friday night, driving Pamela's Volvo. As she got into the car Fiona told her what a lucky girl she was for her dad to buy her a pony. 'I must see it soon.'

At Hawthorn Farm sleep didn't come easily for Heather. She wondered what sort of pony her dad had bought. What colour, what name. She was up early for breakfast on Saturday. Pamela promised to take her to a Cotswold town where the saddler there would fix her up with saddle and bridle. The moment arrived when Bryn Evans's Land Rover and Rice trailer pulled on to the gravel in front of the farmhouse. 'Oh, Daddy! She's beautiful! What's her name?' Heather gasped as the pony was unloaded from the trailer.

Mr Evans told her, 'We call her Bronwyn, but that's Welsh. Call her what you like.'

'Of course not, Mr Evans. Bronwyn it shall be.' Heather then threw her arms around her father's neck and kissed him, saying, 'Thank you Daddy. We break up for Christmas next week, what a lovely Christmas present.'

Bryn Evans looked at the new saddle and bridle and, turning to Lionel, chuckled a bit at such quality, saying, 'That cost a pretty penny but it's worth it.'

'Oh, Mr Evans, that's my wife's doing, she doesn't do things by halves.'

There was no time wasted that Saturday afternoon as Heather rode Bronwyn around the farm field, past old George, who was still working on the boundary wall. 'She's a lucky wench,' he thought to himself with raised eyebrows.

'I want to phone Fiona,' Heather told her mother.

'All right then, Heather, when we have finished tea,' Lionel gave an approving nod.

The phone call revealed the excitement of this young girl with her Christmas present. 'Fiona, the pony is gorgeous. Could I meet you tomorrow on her? Our small field is okay but I'd like to canter around your 100-acre cow ground. I'll meet you tomorrow after lunch at the Tibblestone.'

Fiona replied, 'Oh, Heather! You are a lucky girl. My pony is so ordinary and it sounds as if Bronwyn is so special.'

The two girls circled the 100 acres of the Williams's cow ground. 'Fiona, this afternoon is a day to remember,' laughed Heather.

'Yes, Heather. You're a lucky girl and could be a lady of leisure with a wealthy generous father. You could stay in London, go to the shows, the clubs, and if you marry a farmer, and I know that's what you aim at, Daddy says farming is not such a sure living with surpluses and over production.'

Heather felt a bit put out at Fiona's preaching and answered, 'Now you look here, Fiona. It's not everything to have a generous, rich father, in fact, it can be a drawback. Someone once said the worst thing a farmer can have is too much money. I do know what Daddy has in mind for me, to do show jumping with Bronwyn, but that is not for me.'

With a sigh, Fiona said, 'It's the cowman's half day off. I have to drive the milkers to the parlour, and you, Heather, you must be home before dark.'

'That's true,' Heather replied. 'I know we can spend all our time riding round the 100 acres. I'll give you a hand with the cows, then I must go.'

After that Heather, mounted on Bronwyn, was home at dusk. George, the old retainer, unsaddled the mare and put her in the stable. 'Nice little 'oss you got there. I've checked her over, a six-year-old. I can still recognise quality, you know, Miss, I did my time in the Veterinary Corps in the 'fourteen war. Now anything amiss with Bronwyn, there's no need to send for the Vet.'

'That's kind of you, George, but isn't my pony super?'

'Oh, by the way, Miss, that little pig isn't a runt any more. I expect you've noticed how her's improved. Mary has tended her as if she was a child. It's Boxing Day next week, and the Meet of the Hounds is at the Pear Tree. Shall you be going?'

'I'll see what Fiona says, George, but killing foxes doesn't appeal to me.' Heather went into the kitchen and drank tea with Mary Grafton. It had been a Red Letter Day, free from argument with her parents.

The girls did follow the hounds on Boxing Day for a little while, but Heather hacked back to Hawthorn Farm early in the afternoon. Lionel was giving a supper for the bell ringers in the evening.

CHAPTER EIGHTEEN

CANDLEMAS IN THE
LAMBING PEN
AND HEATHER'S DECISION

Heather was torn between staying at Hawthorn Farm and travelling every day to college, or continuing to be a boarder there. She decided that she should be looking after Bronwyn and Juliet the piglet. A change of heart it's true but, of course, Lionel and Pamela were pleased to have her home and for her to become a day girl at the college. Lionel had been so generous to her and the episode of the scruffy piglet was almost forgotten. Juliet had grown into what George called a gilt, a young sow. She followed Heather from the buildings up onto the top of the Hill on sunny mornings, and there she grazed and rooted on the strong soil. George brought small apples for the little Gloucester Old Spot, some he had sorted out in the harness room. She grunted her approval like the purring of a contented cat. Heather had such a way with animals, so when Juliet saw her at the gate she turned to have her back scratched. When she was old enough Heather thought that it would be marvellous to breed from this young sow, but there were problems.

As Candlemas approached Gwyn Williams's ewes were due to lamb. Heather was drawn like a magnet to the Williams's farm and was welcomed by Gwyn when there was a difficult birth. Her small hands would go more easily into the ewe's passage, and in this way Heather was able to help the farmer. Every weekend she was at the farm, and in the lambing pen in the dry barn. Fiona wasn't so keen on the sheep, 'smelly things' she called them.

'Some of these ewes had difficult births, Mr Williams. What breed was the ram?' Heather commented.

'Oh, I put some to an Oxford tup, you know, a Cotswold type. They have large heads. The ewes are theaves, two years old,' Mr Williams told her.

'Not a ram like the Suffolk with a pointed head?' Heather queried.

'Who told you about Suffolks, Heather?' he asked.

'Well, it's all in the book about sheep breeds, Mr Williams.'

Most of Gwyn's ewes had lambed but one ewe was left. She looked sick, grinding her teeth, twitching her tail and moving around, obviously uncomfortable. Heather and Fiona were with Gwyn, who admitted to young Heather that he was really a dairy farmer who kept a few ewes and was grateful for help with the lambing. 'It's a new enterprise for me, but it's obvious that ewe is not going to deliver on her own. Shall we try Heather or shall I send for the Vet? Heather and Fiona, fetch some hot water from the kitchen and a bar of soap.'

Gwyn knew that modern vets now raise the ewe's back legs, so that the unborn lamb does not press against the passage. So he and Fiona held the ewe more or less on its head, while Heather rolled up her sleeves and, lubricated by soap and water, gently put her little hand into the ewe's passage. Suspecting trouble, Gwyn said, 'Look here, Heather, shall I send for the Vet? I'm sure she has dead lambs inside her. That will put you off.'

Heather replied. 'There's more than one lamb there. I've got hold of a leg, now I must find the head. Good! It's coming! Oh, it's dead.'

The next lamb, a breach birth, was also dead, as was the third. Fiona turned away holding her nose and exclaiming, 'My gosh, doesn't it smell revolting!' Gwyn was dubious of the ewe weathering the ordeal. He put antiseptic into the ewe, and Heather went to Nesta's scullery to wash her hands. But the smell of dead lambs lingered on, a persistent, unbelievable smell.

'Shall I give her some hay, Mr Williams?'

'You can try,' Gwyn answered doubtfully. 'But she won't eat any at present.'

'Oh, I'll try her with ivy. It says in one of my books that sometimes they can be tempted with ivy.'

'You could do, Heather,' and Gwyn, smiling, recited, 'Goats eat ivy, mares eat hay.'

Back at Hawthorn Farm Pamela smelled something nasty as soon as Heather entered the scullery. 'What on earth is that vile smell? Something dead and rotten on your hands? Wash them at once.'

Heather reported that one of Mr Williams's ewes had three dead lambs inside her. 'That's about the last one to lamb. I managed to deliver them, but I'm afraid the ewe may die from inflammation.'

Pamela told her daughter what a stupid girl she was, and that if she had had a wound on her hand it could have become septic, and that Gwyn Williams had an awful cheek to expect her to do his dirty work. 'I'll ring him now,' she added.

Heather pleaded with her mother not to blame Gwyn as he did pay her and had promised to give her two orphan lambs.

As he drove Lionel home in the Rolls from Evesholme station, Phil Grafton pointed out a row of laburnum trees in bloom. Spring had come, and the hedges and fields were at their best. 'Had a good day at the office, Sir?' Phil posed the familiar question to his boss.

'Well, Phil, it's much the same day after day. Investing folk's money, some gain, some lose. You wouldn't like to be involved with stocks and shares. It's been my life, but now at Hawthorn Farm the real world is unfolding.'

'Good night, Sir,' Phil said as Lionel walked from the garage to the house.

In the scullery Heather, with a scrubbing brush, was still washing her hands in disinfectant soap, but Lionel got a whiff of the smell from the kitchen and called out, 'I'm home, Pamela, but what's that awful smell? It's on you, Heather. Go and get changed.'

Pamela described to her husband that the smell was of rotten flesh and that Heather positively stank through delivering dead lambs at the Williams's farm. Lionel, in his usual panic, decided to ring the Vet. 'Hello, is that Alison? I've got a bit of a problem. My daughter has been delivering lambs at Williams's farm and apparently one ewe gave birth to three dead lambs. Her hands stink to high heaven.'

The Vet gave a controlled laugh and said, 'I know, they will smell.'

'That's all very well, Alison, but what is the risk of infection for my daughter?'

The Vet's reply was, 'There is none as long as she uses a good disinfectant, but the smell will be with her for days. Nothing will neutralise it. If it had been a cow that had aborted that would be risky. Don't worry, Mr Bainbridge, your daughter's a brave girl, most farmers send for me with the slightest problems. Gwyn Williams is lucky.'

Lionel and Pamela were secretly pleased that, despite Heather's constant visits to Fiona's father's farm, she had done so well with her exams at the Ladies College. 'She is material for Oxford,' Lionel boastfully announced to his wife over the breakfast table.

'You try and persuade her.' Pamela knew that her daughter was intent on a life spent actively farming the land. At least the Bainbridges were relieved that Heather had not wasted her time at college. Lionel then thought that if she was set on agriculture as a career, perhaps a spell at an agricultural college was worth considering, hoping that she would go to a post with the Ministry, or better still to Brussels, where she could use her brain for the benefit of the EEC.

'Now we have joined the Common Market, or so called, there will be posts going to fight our corner in Europe.'

Pamela sighed. 'It's still only a pipedream, darling. Heather is set on practical farming, I know. Nesta told me aside that girl of ours has a gift with animals.'

'Well, we will see, Pamela. I've a heavy day in Town tomorrow. My God! Everyone goes berserk over the rise in the bank rate. It is a problem.'

One lovely Saturday morning, home from college, Heather was out riding Bronwyn on the slopes of Ayshon Hill. The morning had

been wonderful, the leaves on the beech trees near the folly looked as if they'd been painted in dark gold as the sun scorched the wiry grass. The gorse was still in bloom but now turning to seed pods that made a pleasant little 'popping' noise as Bronwyn's hooves brushed by on the bridle path.

'How glorious, how divine. Just me and my pony away from all the stress of college and home,' Heather thought. 'Dad has a hard life in Town but he enjoys the challenge, always has. I hope he allows me to farm, maybe he will. The skylarks above, singing as they rise in the clear air, the peewits calling, the bumble bees on the boar thistle – don't they tell me something. My life is bent on the land, on nature. Come Bronwyn, one more canter over the wild thyme-carpeted turf then home to lunch, to feed Juliet, and now those two orphan lambs Mr Williams has given me. Mary's a darling, she has them feeding from the bottle. They follow her everywhere.'

As Heather rode into the orchard Old George was chattering to Mary. Your lambs be growing fast, you could wean them now. We allus called the orphan lambs cade lambs, don't know why. Here's young Heather. Had a good ride, Miss? I'll brush Bronwyn down for you. My word, hers all of a muck sweat. Have you been racing her?'

'No, George, but the Hill is steep and it's a warm day, muggy you might say.' In the paddock the young pig met Heather. 'Juliet,' she cried, a signal for the gilt to roll over on her back for her loving owner to stroke the bristly hair on her belly. 'She is growing into a big animal,' Heather said to herself knowing that Gloucester Old Spot pigs develop into quite a size. Juliet, showing off, ran to the slinget by the beech trees. Here she made a shallow furrow, rooting with her snout then grazing the coarse grass of the Hill.

Heather was going to spend the evening with Fiona, and Nesta Williams was picking her up from Hawthorn Farm. Meeting the farmer's wife at the back door, Pamela invited her in for a chat. 'You know how difficult daughters can be, Nesta, have you got problems with Fiona? No doubt she is destined for something in agriculture?'

'Oh no,' came the reply. 'She is not sure yet but says she wants to teach disabled children and she is keen on the scheme now afoot, "Riding for the Disabled". She has an urge to care for the underprivileged.'

With a big sigh, Pamela replied, 'I wonder why we bother so much with their education. That must be a disappointment for you Nesta, when Fiona has such a background. It's the same with Heather. She's absolutely adamant over a farming career. It gets Lionel so mad because with her brain and his influence she could land a career with the Ministry of Agriculture, but no, she prefers to get plastered with cow muck and lambing ewes.'

Nesta, sensing this was a hint from Heather's mother about her working on the Williams's farm, quickly said, 'We must be off. I'll bring Heather back in good time.'

That night, after a happy evening with Fiona, Heather lay wondering why her parents were so intent on her meeting and possibly marrying some city chap. 'They're okay, but not for me,' she thought. 'It's an artificial life in London.' The round of the seasons on Gwyn Williams's farm had altered Heather's view of life for ever. She turned in bed, too tired to sleep, thinking how agriculture was no gold mine, but it was certainly the only way of life that she wanted.

CHAPTER NINETEEN

WHEN THE RABBITS WENT
FROM THE HILL

George Burford and Phil Grafton often spoke of how things were on the Hill before the great rabbit plague of myxomatosis in 1954. George's vegetable garden at Hawthorn Farm was still encircled with the wire netting he had erected to keep the rabbits off his crops. They would have swiped everything, he told Pamela and young Heather one day in spring when the purple-sprouting broccoli gave a dark lilac colour to one part of the garden.

In his time, Phil had been an expert with fruit trees. He recalled how he had put circular wire guards around the trunks of young apple trees in the orchard to prevent the conies, he called them, from nibbling the bark when the snow was on the ground. The Hill was so overrun with rabbits that, to the men who looked over the wall on Spring Hill, it seemed as if the earth moved. It was no trouble to shoot three or four with one shot, George remembered.

'How did it spread, this myxomatosis?' Heather was anxious to learn. She liked all the creatures of the Hill.

'What do you say, Phil? You be more of a scholar than me.'

Phil was a bit hesitant. 'It was VD among the rabbits and 'twas spread by fleas; it started down in Kent. You know the rumours, George.'

George was more outspoken. He would tell tales, rumour or otherwise. 'You know, Miss, the retired Army officer who farmed in the next village, a real old Brass Hat. It's rumoured that he brought a couple of infected rabbits from Kent and turned them out on his farm. He was plagued with rabbits, they grazed his oats and wheat, baring the headlands. Well, this officer had a fall hunting on the Hill. There was a chemist in town, a clever chap, who could cure animals as well as folk. When the officer showed the chemist his damaged arm he said: "Well, I can dress it but are you sure it's not myxomatosis?" This was one way of letting him know what the villagers knew about how the disease spread.'

Phil added that the disease would have come anyway because the whole of Britain was infested apart from a few islands. Then George described what he saw on the Hill when he worked for the Major. 'Rabbits with swollen heads, blinded by disease, would come towards one and I, with pity I suppose, killed them with my stick. It was a terrible sight, unforgettable.'

Heather listened to George as if she was in class at college, but her mother, hearing such things, said, 'I think I'm going to be sick. I'm going back into the house.'

'How did any survive with all that infection?' Heather asked.

Phil Grafton then explained that animals have an instinct. The rabbits stayed on top of the ground in the bushes and just a few kept free of the disease which spread in the burrows. Now they were back but not in such numbers.

'Don't you agree the rabbits were a pest, George?' Heather queried.

'Well, they were too thick on the ground, but you wouldn't remember the war when the meat ration was about 1s 5d per person per week. What was nicer than rabbit stew with onions, carrots and dumplings? That put the hair on my chest during the war.'

A few years after the plague struck the rabbits the village was faced with an arctic winter. It started to snow at tea-time on Boxing Day, when Phil Grafton was driving back from Evesholme after a party. Soon the whole of the Vale and Hill was clothed in white, a colour which one had to get used to for three months.

The severe weather hit the bird population especially hard. The pigeons certainly took a hammering such as they'd never done before in what George Burford called the remembrance of man. A variety of food is available to the pigeons during the short winter days, but this particular winter all food became scarce.

When the land is frozen bone hard and the winter wheat, just a couple of inches high, barely peeps through the snow looking for the spring, pigeons go short on cereal food. Then they relish the berries on the ivy that clings to the brook-side willows. It's a sporting shot when a quice (wood pigeon) with flapping wings flies noisily from the ivy bush, which remains green all the year. But the fruit of the ivy was soon finished by the hungry birds during that arctic winter.

Pigeons do play havoc with the young clover but that winter it too lay under the blanket of snow. Spring cabbage survived for a time but when the icy wind blew the snow away the pigeons and the larks made mincemeat of the young plants. Although one might despair of the damage done by skylarks when hordes of them feed on winter greens, they are now a rare species, and should be spared.

In those years, when the 1939 war was still a vivid memory, the farmers were growing thousands of acres of Brussels sprouts in the Vale and on the Hill. (George Burford once said, 'This parish stinks of sprouts.') That bitter winter, the Brussels sprouts stood on 2-foot stems just above the snow. The sharp frost made picking the sprouts purgatory. Men stood around the bait-time fire under the lea of the hedge, perished with cold. For the pigeons, it was their last chance; hordes descended on the fields and virtually destroyed the crop. Although for a while the frozen buttons had made money in the market, now the pigeons had put paid to the crop on which big growers and little master men depended as their winter harvest.

One had never seen the pigeon suffer before from virtual starvation. They are cunning as a rule and one had to wait in rides for hours sometimes to get the flock in range of the gun. Pigeons died among the sprout rows but they were useless for the pot, starved, as light as a feather. The winter was relentless.

As for the smaller birds, they died in the hedges and fields. Early lambs which were born on the Hill were cased in ice before they were dry. In the coppice the great trees split and, weighed down with ice, crashed to the ground. Some birds roosting in the poplar trees high above the Hill were cased in ice one night after what was known as a glazed frost.

The village of Ayshon was cut off for a while when the bus could not get to the main Evesholme road. A local farmer put a blade on the front of his tractor and tried to bulldoze the snow away, but the wind drifted it back. Most men on the farms were employed in feeding and watering livestock, thawing pipes and sawing wood. Men from the nearby Army camp walked up and down the village street unable to get to work, paid for doing nothing. Some said such a gang with shovels could have made a bus route.

All the greenstuff was finished except some Borecole, or early greens, grown by a neighbour. This stood up to the weather and was eagerly sought in the almost empty vegetable market.

What of the little master men, whose income dried up from January until the spring? Self-employed, they didn't get unemployment pay. Their stamp only covered them for sickness and old age pensions. These were men who worked their smallholdings. Hundreds of them had lost their crops and there was little hope of income for this forgotten army. Their small savings melted like butter in the sun. There was no dole for them, and the old system of 'going on the parish' still smacked of the Poor Law.

So many of these brave hearts went to their doctor. One very well-known practitioner realised their plight. 'What's the problem?' he asked one after another.

'I've got a bad back, Doctor.'

On the bunk as he pushed and pulled at old tired limbs, then, 'On the Panel. Arthritis.'

No one could prove otherwise. These men, had they been able to pick their crops, would have done so despite the arthritis which is common in men who have worked the land. The Panel money kept them going, but in a very restricted way.

The snow and ice of a lifetime provided winter sports for the young and active. The side of the Hill was steep below the Cuckoo Pen. Here the sledges carried their passengers from the top to the bottom hedge and the bridle path. Slides of all kinds, some made from staves of cider barrels, others sophisticated, new from the sports shop in Town. Not exactly the Cresta Run, but here was an opportunity for folk to take advantage of Bredon Hill, which became like a little Switzerland. One mechanically minded chap used the Hill as a ski slope. Finding it hard work ascending back to the top after he had skied down, he fixed a petrol motor to a pulley and made an improvised ski lift.

Les, who owned one of the first Austin Minis in the district, drove to Bredon, carefully tested the ice on the Avon River, and then drove his car along the frozen river to Tewkesbury. Shades of 1898, some of the old worthies said, when they had roasted a pig on the river at Evesholme. Tustin, the coalman, said that was the year there were sixteen weeks of frost in February. A long February!

With the spring came floods from the thawing snow, and markets still very short of produce. The little master men were signed off the Panel. They salvaged parsnips which had been frozen in the ground, and the scant crops of spring onions were, as one grower said, 'like parish churches, one in a place'. It is strange how one of the smallholders' staple crops, known as Gillies, wallflowers, withstood that harsh winter. They were late though, and the women who looked upon Gilly-picking as their first job in the fields, were a month behind making some money.

The clay land which had been dug or ploughed in the late autumn now became what is called a sugar mould: a tilth created by the frost on the land which no implement can copy. Nature has the edge with clay land.

Turnips on the Hill sprouted greens, and anything green was welcome in the markets. The sprout stems that had looked dead now shot forth the greens, so tasty. Men who had left the stems now picked and sold the greens. Spring cabbage ruined by the frost and the pigeons was very scarce, but a few of the growers who planted January King cabbages had a partial crop. Cambridge ring rollers clattered behind the Fordson tractors, firming the winter wheat where the crop was thick, and tethered harrows behind the rollers put weights onto the rollers scattering the young weeds, letting sunshine and light to the wheat plants.

Tragically, the hard winter was too much for some of the old countrymen. The churchyard which held the remains of some thousands of Ayshon ancestors now received more. George Burford had lost so many of his friends over the years, but harked back to Frank Peart's funeral when he was what he called a Boy Chap at Hawthorn Farm. Over his pint in the Old Inn George said to Ted Green; 'Dost remember Old Frank Peart's funeral when we worked for him afore the war?'

'Remember!' Ted exclaimed, 'I'll never forget and you know why. Alf Badger and his brother Jim helped to carry him, all of twenty stone. I forget who the other bearers were. The undertaker as you know had a terrible job to get him in the coffin. The size of his belly.'

'I know,' George said. 'And I saw what you saw as plain as could be. Old Frank's hand was showing under the coffin lid. They couldn't get the lid over it.'

'Oi,' Ted added. 'He's gone to dust now, along of the rest, but what a sight that was!'

CHAPTER TWENTY

THE YFC COMMITTEE MEETING

When Pamela Bainbridge was taking her daughter back to the Ladies College one Monday morning, Heather reluctantly admitted that she was going to a meeting of the Young Farmers' Club in the evening.

'You know, Heather, Phil and I can fetch you home, it's no trouble.'

'That's kind of you, Mother, but one of the members has promised to bring me home after the meeting.'

'Okay then, but not too late, Heather. It does have an effect on your studies.'

Colin Gilder, a young farmer from the Cotswolds, was Chairman of the Club. (He had been thrown in at the deep end of farming after the death of his father, tragically gored by one of their Jersey bulls.) Heather was voted onto the committee and she was delighted, although she felt rather young to take on the office. It was actually Colin who had offered to take Heather home after the meeting. She thought him one of the nicest members of the Club, and it was an extra bonus to be driven home by this nineteen-year-old. The meeting finished at 9 o'clock. 'I'll get you home by 10 o'clock,' Colin promised, 'but would you like fish and chips at Pooles?'

'Okay Colin, but you know Dad and Mum were quite cross when the butcher took me home late. It was the fact that he was *only* a butcher – trade, you know! For a girl from the Ladies College to associate with such a person was not right, you understand? Isn't it funny?'

In Pooles' fish and chip shop, with a glass of squash, Colin said, 'How's that pony of yours? Gwyn Williams told me all about her. I saw him in Gloucester Market on Thursday. He was really impressed by the way you helped with the lambing. Are you taking up farming seriously?'

Heather sighed. 'Oh, I'd love to farm, and at least Dad has agreed for me to go to Hartbury Agricultural College. It was a real struggle for him to agree. Mind you, he hopes for me to get a post with the Ministry of Agriculture. You have no idea what strings Dad can pull. But Ministry posts don't grab me, working with bureaucrats.'

Colin changed the subject, saying, 'You didn't come on the farm walk at the weekend. I believe you had to go to London.'

Heather groaned. 'Please don't remind me of it. Mummy and Daddy were invited to a silver wedding celebration and they tried their damnedest to pair me off with Martin Golding, the son of one of their friends. He's very smooth, goes to Eton and hopes to get into the Diplomatic Corps.'

Colin, laughing, replied, 'You didn't like him, I gather.'

Heather coloured up and raised her voice. 'Like him! He's a wimp and a randy customer. After he had drunk a few whiskies he tried it on. He may have jumped into bed with a few but not with me. I'm never going to sleep with a fellow unless I really love him. I may have to wait but that's worth waiting for, I believe.'

Colin was amused at this girl's determination, and felt that she was worth waiting for too. He laughed loudly and said, 'Come on, Heather. Who's taking you home tonight? Not the 'Bourton Butcher' but me. We must be away, it's 9.30. If we have a drink at the Fox and Hounds you'll still be home by 10 o'clock.'

At the Fox and Hounds an intrigued Heather listened to the local farm men talking about how the spring corn was looking. Some described how the new tractor ploughed with the reversible plough, a far cry from starting and finishing what they called beds, ridging and casting. Colin was more interested in his young companion. He spoke at last. 'Aye, Heather. I haven't got you a drink. I'm having a cider, what's for you?'

Heather speedily replied, 'Oh, just a soft drink, please. I was thinking, these young men haven't had the advantage of higher education but they are so knowledgeable about the land. They speak as if they care for it intimately.'

'You, Heather,' Colin responded, 'also have a feeling for the land, more in livestock, but these tractor drivers in their overalls are very different from what some folk think. The chaps who came before them, in cords and billy cock hats, with their clay pipes, standing by a five-bar gate, that's a memory. . . . Heather . . . ,' Colin sounded as if he had something important to say, ' . . . I'd like to tell you about my father and his death. I rarely speak of it. Do you mind?'

Heather gently replied, 'Please do Colin. I'd like to hear more about your family, although I feel that I know them a little already.'

Colin was somewhat taken aback, then hesitantly began to explain how the Jersey bull, an animal his father had trusted, having reared it from a calf, turned on him in the yard and killed him. Heather, moved to tears, put an arm around the young farmer. 'Oh, Colin, how awful. I'm glad you told me and that you trust me as a friend.'

Colin reassured her, 'That is what life is all about, but Heather, an evening with you tells me something, dare I say it? I think I love you already.'

This time it was Heather's turn to be startled. She blushed, to be more precise she glowed, and she leant over to kiss his cheek and whispered. 'I've never loved a boy before, but you are a darling and yes, I think I love you too. Tell me more about your family, your farm, your mother.'

'You must come over to tea and meet Mother. You know we live at the Wren's Nest at the hamlet of Ramacre. Since Dad's death, Mother's done bed and breakfast. I milk seventy Jersey cows and rear a few pedigree Jersey calves as Dad did. I've got a boy to help me. I'm sure Mother will like you.' Thinking aloud, he added, 'She had better.'

The couple were home at Hawthorn Farm by 10.20 and, after a quick 'Good Night' to Heather, Colin drove down the drive. Pamela and Lionel were having a nightcap in the lounge. Pamela met her daughter in the hall, greeting her with, 'Who was that who brought you home, Heather? Quite a smart young man – at least he looked more presentable than that butcher off the Cotswolds.'

Heather gave a careful, somewhat guarded reply. 'He's the Chairman of the Young Farmers and farms at the Wren's Nest at Ramacre. He and his mother have a herd of Jersey cows.'

Lionel was listening in the doorway. Clearing his throat, he bellowed, 'Jerseys! Jerseys! He's backing a wrong one there. All this new talk of cholesterol! Most sensible folk will be drinking semi-skimmed milk soon you know.'

Heather responded, 'Oh, Daddy, for goodness sake! Lots of folk still like cream. They buy Gold Top milk from the Channel Island cows. Take George Burford, for instance. He's in his seventies, eats masses of fat bacon, and he's fit enough.'

Lionel was unimpressed. Ignorant of farming trends, he gruffly changed the subject. 'It's time for bed . . . but I do think the farmers should stand on their own two feet instead of being propped up with subsidies.'

Still glowing from the events of the evening, Heather replied, 'Good night, Daddy and Mummy. Thank you for allowing me to go to the agricultural college next term. You won't regret it.'

It was a perfect Saturday afternoon in early summer when Colin came to pick up Heather to take her to the Wren's Nest. Heather was anxious about meeting Colin's mother; perhaps Mrs Gilder would not like having to share her son's affections. The two had lived together since the death of her husband. 'Who is this girl who's taking my son from me?' she might think.

But Heather need not have worried. The welcome at the farm was so warm and very sincere. 'Oh, Colin's told me about you. Come in, dear. I've picked my first strawberries from the garden. We shall have them for tea with cream. I've heard how you helped Gwyn Williams with the lambs.'

Heather smiled. 'Oh, that's nothing. Colin does exaggerate. I'm very naive really about things concerning farming, a beginner you understand, Mrs Gilder, but anxious to learn.'

'Well, Heather, some folks think that women know nothing about the care of animals but, believe me, men can be rough with calves. I've had to manage since Colin's dad's death. Life has to go on, and Colin is a good lad.'

The three farming folk sat down to tea on the lawn under the damson trees in the cool of the afternoon. As soon as tea was over Colin got up to go and change into his working clothes ready for milking. Heather wondered out loud, 'Could I help him with the milking.'

Mrs Gilder, who reasoned that she could not work in her pretty dress, promised to lend her something to wear, but Heather explained, 'It's no problem. I've brought a shirt and jeans, all my working stuff. Can I go and change somewhere? My wellies are in Colin's car.'

When Heather reappeared in her working clothes, Colin called from the yard. 'I didn't expect you to work, Heather. You can stay and talk to Mother. I must say that you looked smashing in that dress, but jeans are better for the cowshed.'

Heather laughed. 'We'll have no more of that, young farmer. Let's get the milking done, there are two of us now.'

After tuition with Gwyn Williams, Heather surprised Colin with the deft way she slipped the machine on the teats of the Jerseys, and the job was done in just over an hour. As she looked around the young stock, a young Jersey bull caught Heather's eye. 'That's going to the Three Counties Show at Malvern,' Colin told her.

As Heather washed and changed in the bathroom Mrs Gilder had a chance to talk to her son. 'What a nice girl, Colin, no side on her and you did say her father is a big man in the city. Bring her here any time you can, Colin, she's so natural and your Dad would have been so proud of you and your friend.'

It was getting dark when the couple left the Wren's Nest for Hawthorn Farm. 'Do you mind if we take a longer route home, Heather? It is such a lovely evening.'

Heather squeezed Colin's arm as he held the steering wheel. 'Anywhere with you, but we must be home in good time.'

'Okay, darling. Oh! Do you mind me calling you that? It just slipped out.'

'Don't be so silly, Colin. I like it.'

Colin drove up the Cotswold Edge, through Broadway, until they reached the eighteenth-century tower. The moon came up as huge as a wagon wheel, casting shadows over the thyme-covered turf. Holding each other, looking towards the Vale, Colin marvelled at how many counties could be seen from there in daylight, and how the lights of the Malverns were like beacons guiding planes to the airfield beyond Bredon below.

He murmured gently in Heather's ear, 'Oh, it's bliss to hold you, to put my arms around you. I feel we shall never part, two kindred spirits together in the moonlight.'

As they kissed Heather sighed, and whispered, 'I trust you Colin, you lovely man.' She was so beautiful to hold that night, and Colin, daringly, slipped his hand under her dress and wondered what she might say as his hand rested on her breast. She cried out, 'That's lovely, but do be careful.'

Conscious of her quickened heartbeat, Colin knew that the love was mutual, that they were indeed in tune. The feeling they shared was one that they had longed for, but Heather was firm – so far and no further.

As the car wound its way through the woods Colin turned to Heather and said, 'Promise me, my darling Heather, that we will explore these hills again.'

Heather replied, 'That's an easy promise to keep. There is a bond already, a bond which I will not break.'

At Hawthorn Farm Lionel invited Colin into the lounge where he had been watching a play on television. 'Come on in and have a drink. You are a farmer, I gather. I know very little about farming, but aren't farmers for ever complaining?'

'Yes, we are,' Colin replied. 'So often everything is right, then the weather spoils it all. But it's a gamble I enjoy.'

'Well, thank you for bringing my daughter home at a respectable hour.'

As Colin left Hawthorn Farm, Heather thanked him for such a lovely evening and said to thank his mother too for the tea. Back in the lounge Pamela did her usual quizzing. 'Do you like Colin?'

'Yes I do, but I hardly know him yet. His mother is rather sweet. It's so tragic that her husband was killed by a bull.'

Lionel retorted sharply, 'I warned you about bulls. I was worried when you handled one of Gwyn Williams's, and that was a Hereford. I gather Jerseys are more unpredictable than Herefords.'

Heather then told her parents, 'Colin has a young bull he's taking to the Three Counties Show and it's a beauty. He has shown me how to groom it. I would like to go to the Show.'

Lionel was too annoyed about bulls to carry on arguing about them. He said instead, 'Well, when you go to Hartbury College you'll discover that farming isn't all beer and skittles, like the Young Farmers' Club. You'll learn the economics of Agriculture to prepare for a Ministry job. I met a chap from the Ministry of Agriculture at my club the other week and he said there are excellent prospects for posts in the Ministry. You may have to take a course at Reading University. That is important.'

Heather shrugged her shoulders and replied, 'Let's take one step at a time, Daddy.'

CHAPTER TWENTY-ONE

BRUCELLOSIS

George Burford was a stickler for punctuality. He always arrived at Hawthorn Farm on the dot of 7.30, one could have set the clock by this pensioner. He always had a cup of tea from Pamela before starting work. One Monday morning Pamela and Phil Grafton were concerned. Half past eight came and Pamela said to the chauffeur/gardener, 'There's still no sign of George.'

Phil had just returned from Evesholme after taking Lionel to catch the early morning train. 'Go round to his cottage, Phil, and see if he's all right. I do need my tomatoes picked in the greenhouse, but that's not important. It's George that worries me. I hope he's all right. You know, living alone, and at his age, anything could have happened. He may have fallen. Just see if he needs anything.'

'I'll go now, Mrs Bainbridge,' Phil said. 'Not to worry.' He returned from George's cottage in about twenty minutes, all smiles.

'Is he all right, Phil?'

'Yes, Ma'am. A bit under the weather. He says that he'll be okay by Wednesday after a rest, but he just needs to put his feet up. He says there's no need to send for a doctor.'

On Wednesday morning George arrived at Hawthorn Farm as Phil said, as bright as a button. Pamela greeted him with a cup of tea, asking, 'Are you better? Did you have that 24-hour 'flu that's going around?'

George's reply shocked Pamela. 'No Ma'am, 'twas nothing like that. It was the brucellosis. I get a recurrence of it occasionally.'

'What on earth are you saying, George?' she exclaimed. That's contagious abortion. You haven't got that for sure. You are joking, aren't you?'

George told Pamela that he was quite serious. 'I caught it from a cow which slipped her calf when I was working on the farm fifty years ago. Every now and then I have a temperature and have to stay with my feet up for a couple of days. There's no cure for me. Lots of vets have the complaint, and lots of stockmen.'

He went on to explain that when a cow aborts she is a long time cleansing and retains the after-birth. 'I caught it from there, perhaps it got into my blood through a cut in my hand when the cow needed attention. It's nothing really, Ma'am. It's now a thing of the past, for herds have to be attested 'cos with brucellosis the milk may cause trouble. It's a risk we took years ago.'

Pamela had turned white, and burst into tears, crying out, 'Oh, George, how awful, and Heather has worked with the Williams's cows and now with Colin Gilder's herd. She may be infected. Oh, I wish that Heather had never met the Williams's or his cows. What can I do? I'm not blaming you, George, but to think that you've suffered for fifty years. This is the worst thing that's happened to our family.'

George was nonplussed, wondering how he could pacify his mistress. He gently said, 'Don't distress yourself, Ma'am. There's no risk today now herds are accredited. I'm still here.'

Pamela ran into the kitchen to see Mary, telling her that something dreadful had happened and that George had been ill with brucellosis. Heather had been with Williams's cows and with Colin Gilder's, and now she may have brucellosis. Mary tried her best to comfort Pamela, assuring her that both the Williamses and the Gilders had accredited herds.

On the phone to Heather at college Pamela told her the bad news about George and that she was beside herself with worry about Heather. 'What can I do, Heather? You may well be infected and have this thing all your life. George says there's no cure.'

Heather's reply was not convincing to her mother, but she simply said, 'There's nothing to worry about now that all herds are tuberculin tested and accredited, which means they're free from brucellosis. All reactors are slaughtered. No milk producer is allowed to sell milk otherwise.'

But Pamela insisted, 'I'm coming to Cheltenham and will pick you up at lunch-time and make an appointment with our Doctor for you to see him. See you at 12.30.'

Pamela was still very agitated when she and her daughter arrived at the Doctor's surgery. In the car-park she made yet another assumption regarding the possible infection of brucellosis. 'You know, Heather, sometimes you do have a slight temperature, and I really am worried about the risk you are taking in the milking parlour.'

Heather laughed out loud saying, 'Oh, Mother! Surely that's the curse, isn't it every month?'

'Please! I don't like you being so indelicate. The curse indeed! I suppose mixing with farming people gives you that coarseness. It's not lady-like.'

At the surgery Pamela longed for proof from the Doctor that Heather had not been at risk. She began telling him how worried she was that Heather had been working with cows, and that George, her handyman, had brucellosis which he contracted fifty years ago, and that it recurs now and again. 'Oh dear, Doctor.'

'Now Mrs Bainbridge, I can assure you there's nothing to worry about. There was a slight risk years ago before cows were attested. Farmers have to comply with strict regulations today.' Pamela was hard to convince. 'Would you give Heather a blood test?'

But the Doctor was adamant. 'There's absolutely no need for that, and it would prove nothing.'

Still not wholly believing the Doctor, Pamela was in an anxious state when Lionel returned home that evening. He had already been told by Phil about old George's brucellosis as they travelled the 6 miles from Evesholme station. He burst into the hall, and was hanging his overcoat and trilby on the stand as Pamela met him. 'What's this Phil has told me about old George and brucellosis?'

Pamela, in tears, flung her arms around Lionel, crying, 'Oh, darling, I've been in a state since George came this morning. Even though Heather has helped with the calves, the Doctor says there's no risk and that the disease is virtually wiped out.'

Lionel, still really the city gent, was dubious of country ways. He said to his wife, 'I wouldn't trust farmers any further than I could spit. They are unscrupulous, all they think about is profit. I wouldn't be surprised if some of their herds are full of brucellosis. I'm going to my Club tonight. George Sims, a senior officer from the Ministry of Agriculture will be there. I may get some sense from him.'

At the Conservative Club in Town there was a good mix of professional men, and a few farmers. Lionel had been accepted as bringing new ideas to the provincial town, and was known by some as one of the more respectable stockbrokers from the city. That evening he was in no mood for socialising. He wanted an opinion from George Sims from the Ministry of Agriculture.

George bought him a drink at the bar, remarking, 'You don't look your usual self tonight, Lionel. Something on your mind?'

'I needed that drink, George. We are in a state of worry at home. Our daughter has been working with a neighbour's cows, The old boy who is our handyman has revealed that he suffers from brucellosis that he caught off some cows fifty years ago.'

George could see how serious Lionel felt about the risk but could only tell him what the Doctor had told Pamela. 'The disease is virtually extinct. It was rife fifty years ago. The milk from infected cows then went into manufacturing. Now reactors are slaughtered. Herds have to be accredited. Mind you, we at the Ministry have to keep an eye on some farmers in case they fail to report any reactors. As for risks to your daughter, there are none.'

Lionel believed George Sims, but was annoyed that Pamela had been put to such anxiety. 'Have another drink, Lionel,' George suggested.

He agreed, adding, 'I suppose Phil can fetch me tonight in Pamela's Volvo. I'm not going to Town tomorrow.'

George Sims was one contact whom Lionel felt could be valuable to the family. He had already met Heather and judged her as good material for a management job. 'Now, look here, Lionel,' he began, over the next drink. 'For God's sake, your daughter, I'm sure, has more potential than spending her time up to her ankles in manure. When she finishes her training I promise you I'll get her a good post with us at the Ministry. We work closely with the EEC in Brussels, and the scope there for a bright girl is enormous. I've only a few more years to do in London but, by God! I'd be over there if I was a young man.'

Phil arrived about 10.30 to pick up his boss, who told George Sims that they would keep in touch, and that he must bring his wife over to Hawthorn Farm one weekend.

CHAPTER TWENTY-TWO

HARTBURY COLLEGE

On Heather's seventeenth birthday Lionel, as generous as ever, bought her a new Ford Fiesta car and paid for her to have a course of driving lessons in Cheltenham. Colin smiled as he accompanied the learner driver around Gloucestershire's 'B' roads. 'It's not usual for a learner to pass the test first time,' he teased.

These words from her boyfriend made Heather more determined than ever to be an exception to the rule. The day came, after only a month at the wheel, when the examiner told her she could throw away the L-plates. It was an added bonus to young Heather, for her course at Hartbury Agricultural College started a week later.

The fact that her daughter could travel to and from college and Hawthorn Farm every day pleased Pamela, who had been willing to do the driving if Heather had failed her test, and of course Lionel was also pleased. He still had mixed feelings about Hartbury, but expected it would be a stepping-stone to Reading University, after which he hoped Heather would get a plum job with the Ministry of Agriculture. Before she started her course at the college, Lionel had a heart-to-heart talk with his daughter. 'This should be a good beginning for you, a step towards an administrative post at the Ministry. It's not what your Mother and I had in mind for you. A spell at an academy in Paris would have broadened your mind, and we always imagined you in a more artistic role rather than agriculture, but work hard, dear, and when you have graduated at Reading University doors will surely open for you.'

Heather knew how her dad felt and realised that he wanted her to be in administration rather than the practical side of agriculture. She was bent on animal health and being in charge of a herd where the Vet is seldom called, reminding her father that in these days progressive farmers gave injections to ailing animals themselves.

Lionel tried one final fling before his daughter took to the wide world of college. 'Well, my girl, you're still so young; my instincts are that there's more reward to be had in administration.'

The first day at Hartbury was an anxious day for all the new students. Heather had the benefit of what she had learned at the Williams's farm, but that was not academic. She found the students a mixture; some were sons and daughters of farmers and some were very keen town folk taking their first step on the farming ladder.

Heather pondered the dilemma that while she aimed at practical farming, her dad had only let her take this course in preparation for Reading University, and a post with the Ministry of Agriculture. 'It smacks of the Civil Service,' she thought, 'and my idea is practical farming with animals. Oh, paperwork farming, I know there's no job satisfaction in that for me.'

After an eye-opening week at college studying blood lines in animals, milk yields, and so forth, Heather drove to the Wren's Nest and Colin. As her car drew up, the young farmer in his overalls, met her. He threw his arms around her and kissed her. 'How was your first week at Hartbury? I've been so concerned about you and expected a phone call. My God! It's so good to see you. How I've missed you. Come in! Mother's making tea.'

Heather agreed that she should have rung. 'But studying takes so much time, and in the evening when I'm back at Hawthorn Farm I'm shattered. Are you all right, dear?'

Colin replied that he was very much all right now he had seen her, and that it was the Young Farmer's barbecue that night at the Williams's farm. 'You know that, and you will come with me, of course?'

Putting on an important-sounding voice, Heather replied 'Yes; don't forget I'm still a committee member of the Young Farmers' Club. Now look, I mustn't drive my car after dark, I've promised Daddy that, so I'll drive home to Hawthorn Farm and you can pick me up from there in your car. *Then* we can stay out late! I feel like spending a really long time with you, Colin, and would like to be with you for ever, that's one thing for sure.'

Colin felt a little shy at this outburst. He replied, 'My precious, my love for you is more than anything in the world. I've been so worried in case some student vamped you last week. Call me possessive if you like. I'm sorry, but I may be.'

Heather, happy beyond words, whispered into Colin's ear, 'Don't get silly ideas in your head. It's you I love and you only. Come here, darling, just one kiss and I'll be off. Thank your mother for the tea.'

Mrs Gilder, looking from her kitchen window, said to herself, 'That's my future daughter-in-law. I've prayed for this.'

At Hawthorn Farm about an hour later, Colin arrived to pick up his young lady and Pamela was soon on the scene, tactless as ever. 'Heather tells me you have a milking herd. Have any of your cows had brucellosis?'

Colin thought to himself 'What a greeting!' He took his time to reply. 'Good heavens no! We have an accredited herd, pedigree Jerseys. Dad started with a dozen cows thirty years ago from stock brought from the Channel Islands.'

Lionel came into the hall. He asked Colin, 'Are you a local man? Where did you go to school?'

Colin was quite pleased with his achievements, and said, 'Northleach Grammar School. I think it has gone Comprehensive now. I got a couple of 'A' levels, then Dad needed me on the farm when I was seventeen.'

Obsessed with university education, Lionel replied, 'That's a pity. You could have gone to university. A university education is necessary even for farmers today.'

As Heather sat by Colin in the car on the way to the barbecue Colin was very quiet. Heather guessed what was wrong and said, 'Never mind. That was a bit galling what Daddy said about university. I'm sorry he's like that.'

Colin told her, 'I am sure that your Dad doesn't want me for a son-in-law, but we'll see when the time comes.' Suddenly, he laughed out loud. Heather was curious, for he had been so quiet.

'Why the laugh?' she asked.

'I think your dad was so funny when he said "even farmers should have a university education". Even farmers, as if they were a different species!

But by now Heather's thoughts were miles away. Colin had said something that she was pondering over. 'Colin, what did you mean when you said "we'll see when the time comes" after your rather definite comment that Dad didn't want you for his son-in-law? It's a funny proposal, but I'm so happy you think that way.'

Now it was Heather's turn to laugh, and it was hard to resist throwing her arms around the young farmer as he drove towards the Williams's farm. At last she said, 'It was the funniest of proposals and it meant more to me than if you had asked me to marry you on bended knee. It means that Daddy is not going to rule our lives. I'll marry you, of course I will – "when the time comes"!'

As Colin drove the car into the Williams's yard, the glow of the barbecue already shone from the orchard, lighting up the scene. Colin gave Heather the most passionate kiss she had ever had from him and said, 'Will you marry me? Let there be no mistake about my clumsy proposal.'

Heather replied, 'Oh, I've missed you this week and, of course I'm yours, yours alone, and I promise to be your wife and that we will not be apart so long again.'

Heather's friend Fiona was at the barbecue. She introduced Colin to Gwyn Williams, who remembered meeting him at market and reminded him how Heather had been a midwife to some of his lambing ewes, and had saved him a packet on vet's bills.

After meeting more friends and having coffee in Nesta Williams's kitchen, the couple had so much to talk about and left quite early. 'Where shall we go, Heather? I don't fancy a pub tonight, beer swilling and tobacco smoke. The moon is full, it's a lovely evening.'

Heather knew where she and Colin could be away from the madding crowd. 'Darling, take me to the folly high on the hill. We can sit on that seat at the foot of the tower and see the lights twinkling in the Vale below. It's magic up there.'

At the tower the moon shone almost as bright as day. Even the sea mist failed to dim the twinkling lights of the Malvern Hills. The wooden seat below the tower was a viewpoint for the couple, a love nest. Heather spoke at last. 'You know, I feel much nearer to God up here than I do in church. Speak to me again, Colin, of the future. I feel that to stay up here with you would be everlasting bliss.'

'Oh, Heather. I love you so much. Perhaps it's possessive, but I'm really jealous of you being among all those chaps at Hartbury. Do you really like any of them?'

As Heather threw her arms around her true love and kissed him passionately, tears rolled down her cheeks as she sobbed, 'I'm not looking for anyone else. You mean everything to me. One chap named Michael has been chatting to me. His father's a judge in Birmingham. But he's got a girlfriend, he's just someone to talk to in the canteen. His father wanted him to take up law but he's another one who got away and intends to farm.'

Colin so wished that he was at Hartbury, spending day after day with Heather. He said, 'Promise me, Heather, not to tell your parents about this chap. His father's a judge and they'll try to push him onto you. They don't like me you know, just because I've never been to public school and I work on the land.'

Heather's response was to take him in her arms and say, 'Now come here, darling. This night spent under the moon is special to us both; let's keep it that way. Put your head on my shoulder and relax and I'll lie in your arms. Love conquers all, you know. You've won my heart, darling. I'm still giggling inside remembering your proposal. "When the time comes" you said, will you marry me, and the answer is yes. Does that make you happy, my dearest.'

The kisses lingered, at first passionate then very gentle. 'Is that better now, Colin?'

He was silent for a moment with young Heather Bainbridge safely in his arms. 'Oh, how I long to be able to love you all night long.'

Heather's reply was the same as ever, yet a reply so difficult to maintain. 'You know, Colin, you said "when the time comes". It will come soon. Isn't this a wonderful place? The mist below gives the feeling that we're alone on an island, a beautiful desert island, a thousand feet above the sea, under the stars and that mocking moon, looking down as the Vale below moves in like the waves on the sea. Just look again at that moon. . . .'

Colin had left his car some distance from the tower alongside a coppice of beech trees. As the couple were halfway back a vixen squealed like a child. Colin's grip on the girl tightened and he said softly, 'It's okay, darling. Just a vixen out hunting for her supper.'

A golden plover, known to country folk as a whistling plover, called as it passed high above the hill. 'Someone's whistling at us, Colin,' Heather laughed as the church clock below struck twelve.

Back in the car Colin checked his watch by the light when he opened the door. 'It is 12 o'clock. I wondered whether I had miscounted the striking church clock in the Vale. Whatever will your dad say, out this late. We must hurry home.'

Heather replied, 'I just don't care any more and somehow it seems to me that Dad's a little less possessive.'

Colin said, 'I know. But he doesn't like me, so even if I'd taken you home earlier it would make no difference. I may as well be killed for a sheep as a lamb!'

It was a quick 'good night' in the porch of Hawthorn Farm, and as Heather crept to her bedroom Pamela called, 'Good night, Heather. You are awfully late. Daddy's asleep.'

Heather replied quietly, 'I've had a super time.'

At college the next day Heather's mind was on Colin, on the farm with his Jersey herd. To her he was everything, a rural prince with such gentle ways. She had made plans for how she could help him when they were married. At lunch-time Colin phoned, a voice she longed to hear. 'Just to say how much I love you, and thanks for last night. I have a favour to ask from you, Heather. I've entered a bull for the Three Counties Show. Would you parade him around the ring for me? Ladies often do and you'd look absolutely gorgeous with your blonde hair falling in curls over the collar of a white smock, so different from the other women.'

Heather laughed. 'It's the bull they will be judging, not me, but I'll be so proud to go on parade. I have told Mummy and Daddy that I'm going to the Show with you, but that I'll be walking your bull around the ring is a secret between just you and me. I'll be over this evening to help you. Have you cut any mowing grass yet?'

'Do come tonight. I don't expect to work, the milking will be done and the boy will help me. Mind, if you want to help me groom the bull, that's okay. A woman's touch you know! I'm mowing 10 acres next week. Oceans of love. Bye until tonight.'

After a hurried meal that evening Heather walked to her car ready to go to the Wren's Nest. Pamela called from the front door across the drive. 'Are you seeing Colin this evening? Your Daddy and I think you are chasing after him too much. Make yourself hard to get is my advice, and please don't arrange anything for Sunday. The Rector has asked us over to tea.'

Heather waved to her mother and promised not to arrange anything, shouting, 'I like Revd Lamb, he's a sweety, but tonight I'm helping Colin to get his bull ready for the Show.'

Overhearing the conversation, Lionel shouted loudly. 'Another blasted bull. You are the limit!'

At the Wren's Nest Colin had started to groom the young bull. It was in a loose box, tied with a halter to a ring in the wall. As Heather arrived Colin wasted no time but threw his arms around her. Heather was a bit startled and said jokingly, 'Now my lad, there's work to be done. Still, it's nice to know someone loves me.'

Colin asked if she would hold a bucket of water under the animal's tail so that he could wash it and make it what he called 'feathery'. 'You won't trim the tail, Colin?' she wondered.

He replied, 'Ever so slightly. Now we will give him a shampoo and comb the hair on his top knot. After that, I'll change and we can go somewhere if you like, Heather.'

'Anywhere with you! But can you really spare the time? Somewhere perhaps by the river, aye?'

Colin considered the situation. 'Well, I've a heifer starting to calve so we mustn't go too far or stay too long, as she may have problems, but a little walk by the riverside, perhaps the source of the Windrush. What's 15 miles in the car?'

It was a lovely evening in June, nearing the longest day, and the night sounds and smells of early summer in the countryside were breathtaking. Colin slipped a bottle of cider into the boot of the car. He knew a place where the spring water would cool the drink. Seeing her escort with the bottle, Heather commented, 'Steady on, Colin, that's a quart. I mustn't drink too much, you know. I have to drive home from the Wren's Nest.'

Knowing that parting was so painful, Colin replied, 'You have to drive home! Oh, for the time when "home" is with me, and we can be together in each other's arms.'

A kiss from Heather said everything as she whispered, 'Be patient, darling. It won't be long now.'

The young couple walked by the Old Mill where the mowing grass was knee-deep by the riverside. On the other side of the stream horse beans were in bloom, the intoxicating scent mingling with that of the wild honeysuckle. Heather stopped and drank in the perfume, saying quietly, as if someone would overhear, 'Who needs scent out of a bottle? It's all here, so lovely.'

Colin stared at the water. After a long pause, he replied, 'Let's walk to the source of the river where it's fed by those Cotswold springs and watch the trout.'

At the source of that meandering river, where the water oozes from the limestone, Colin spread a rug on the grass and the couple sipped cider in turns from the bottle. The place was so far away from human habitation that the quietness could be felt. They were just a couple of lovers under a June sky, with the larks above and the peewits calling, protecting their nests.

As Colin caressed her so lovingly Heather winced and sighed, 'No more, Colin. We will wait until our wedding night. Oh, Colin, how hard it was for me to say that.'

Colin's kiss and his words were reassuring. 'Of course, I agree. I love you too much to upset you more.'

Heather lay on the blanket, imagining it to be their wedding night bed and saying softly, as if the stream should not hear, 'It's idyllic here. Darling, thank you for loving me in this heavenly place. I'll dream and dream of this spot and of you.'

Colin held her so tight that he felt her soft breasts pressing against his chest. 'We are so close,' he murmured. 'So close.'

Heather seemed deep in thought. When she finally spoke, she changed the subject. 'Have you ever wondered at how clear this water is before it reaches London, where it becomes so polluted, . . . oh, just look at those dragonflies! Aren't they gorgeous, gossamer and all colours! Listen, is that a coot or a moorhen?'

Colin assured her that it was a moorhen, and she was with her chicks on a little island of weeds. As they drank the last of the cool cider, Colin suggested that they really should be off home, but asked Heather for just one promise.

'Oh, Colin, I'll try,' she said.

'Will you promise that you won't let any other chap be intimate with you? Oh, my God, you're such a temptation and all those college chaps will recognise that. Please keep the first bite of the apple for me.'

Heather laughed so loudly that the peewits made angry calls and the moorhen, followed by her chicks, swam to the other bank of the stream. 'Silly boy!' she said, pulling him towards her. 'Is that really worrying you? What a worrier you are! I suppose it's being a farmer, nothing is certain on the land.'

Back at the farm buildings Mrs Gilder met the couple in the yard, telling them that the heifer had started to calve. As Colin looked into the pen he saw the heifer unsettled, but with the knowledge of a man of experience he said, 'She will be a little while yet.'

Mrs Gilder chipped in with a humorous comment. 'Your Dad always said "when the apple is ripe it will fall".'

That made young Heather think thoughts of full commitment with the man she loved so passionately, of how wonderful it would be to marry him and to have his baby. 'When the apple is ripe it will fall,' she mused.

The evening in June had to come to an end. At a quarter to ten the signs of the closing of the day showed in the big red sun beginning to hide below the Malverns. Heather sighed. 'I must be off home. I would have liked to stay until the heifer calved, but you may be with her until midnight and I must be home before dark.'

'I'll see you on the day of the Show,' said Colin. 'If you drive over to the Wren's Nest you can come with me in my car. I'm taking the yearling bull in the trailer. . . . Oh no, that won't do. Come to the Show in your car because I'll have to stay there overnight. I've bought you a nice white smock to wear. I reckon I know your size. I should do by now! It's 12 isn't it?'

Heather replied, 'How sweet of you. I'll wear one of the cotton blouses you like, some woollen stockings, and brown brogue shoes.'

As Heather drove away Colin ran along by the car, saying his good nights through the open window. 'Good night, my love. I won't let you out of my sight at the Show. Too many Young Farmers around. Of course, I'm only jealous; you should be pleased really.'

Heather's final words were. 'I am, Colin. Goodbye.'

CHAPTER TWENTY-THREE

THE THREE COUNTIES SHOW

At the Three Counties Show Colin's bull took second prize in its class. He eagerly awaited Heather's arrival after the judging. When she came into the ring she noticed by the bull's rosette that it had been placed second. 'Not First then, Colin? Why?'

Colin explained that the champion came from the AI Centre and was worth an awful lot of money, and that he might use its semen, when it was available, on his cows. 'I'm quite pleased, Heather, and delighted that you're going to parade my bull around the ring later in the afternoon. The Herefords take precedence, of course, being a native breed. You will follow the Friesians. There are a lot of Friesians.'

'Oh, Colin! Heather replied, 'I just can't wait. I'm so looking forward to the parade, and you know your bull behaved beautifully when we took him around the orchard at the Wren's Nest. He's used to me now. I could lead him on the halter, but as you say, he must be on a bull stick because of the other animals.'

The parade took place in front of a good crowd. Maybe Colin was biased but he reckoned that the biggest applause, the loudest clapping, came as Heather passed in front of the grandstand. Of course, the young bull behaved perfectly, but a big Ayrshire needed two stockmen to hold him on two bull sticks as a precaution.

The usual newspaper reporters came, including a cameraman from the local paper, all wanting to know about the young herdswoman. A photograph for the *Farming Press* was taken of Heather holding the bull. When a reporter asked where she lived and about her family background it slipped out that her father was a well-known stockbroker, not a stock breeder – Lionel Bainbridge of Hawthorn Farm, Ayshon.

As Heather returned to Ayshon her head was in such a whirl. Pamela met her in the garden.

'Oh yes, Mummy! I've had a good day at the show.' She thought, 'Oh, my God, I'm glad I've left the smock in Colin's car.'

'You are coming to the Rectory on Sunday?' Pamela asked.

'Of course I am, and I'm looking forward to it,' Heather replied.

As Phil Grafton met the London train at Evesholme station he found Lionel pretty tired after a hectic day in the office. As he drove the Rolls back home he simply said, 'Good evening, Sir' and no more. But Lionel seemed keen to talk and said:

'There's a lot of extra work in the Stock Market. Every Tom, Dick and Harry is buying and selling. Is it a bad thing, Phil?'

'I don't know, Sir,' he replied.

Pamela, as bright as a button, welcomed her husband with, 'Dinner's nearly ready.' She looked at the tired man and thought again. 'Perhaps you would like to unwind in the lounge with a drink.'

Lionel agreed and asked, 'Has the *Echo* come yet?'

Pamela replied, 'I'll fetch it for you. I heard the boy put it through the letter-box.'

As Lionel perused the paper one item of news sent fire through his body. He shook and shouted, 'Pamela, come here. Have you seen this? Just listen! Our daughter's photograph, holding Colin Gilder's bull at the Three Counties Show. The paper and young Gilder will hear about this. I'll read it to you.

The Second Prize for Jerseys was won by Colin Gilder of the Wren's Nest, Ramacre, with his yearling bull. In the picture: Heather Bainbridge, who led Mr Gilder's bull around the show ring. Miss Bainbridge, who is studying at Hartbury Agricultural College, lives at Hawthorn Farm, Ayshon. Her father is a well-known stockbroker, senior partner in Bainbridge and Matthews in the city.

'What a blasted cheek to bring my name into it when I wanted some privacy here. We shall have every Tom, Dick and Harry up here now, asking "What shall I invest in, Mr Bainbridge?" I need privacy at home. These flaming reporters wheedling my name from our Heather.'

Heather was at the Wren's Nest. Lionel immediately ran to the telephone and dialled. Colin answered the telephone. Lionel told him that he wanted a word with him after speaking to his daughter. Heather, sensing something wrong, came to the phone. 'Hello, Daddy. You seem annoyed. What's the matter?'

Lionel gasped, 'What's the matter! Everything is the matter my girl. Your picture's in the *Echo* and why did you mention my name? I don't want every prying cove in Gloucestershire to know my address.'

Heather explained as gently as she could. 'I am sorry, Daddy, but it slipped out to the reporter when he asked me. He was such a nice chap, interested in farming.'

Lionel snapped. 'Let me speak to Colin.'

Colin took the phone from Heather. 'Hello, Sir. I'm sorry about the report in the paper.'

Lionel was still very annoyed. 'I want to talk about something else.'

Colin whispered to Heather, 'Oh dear, what have I done now?'

Lionel continued, 'You've got my daughter to lead your bull

around the showground. It's highly dangerous with crowds of folk around. You have no right to take advantage of a girl under eighteen, and my responsibility, without a by your leave from me. Understand? And another thing, she's spending too much time with you instead of studying.'

Colin replied, 'I'm sorry you feel like that. Heather did ask me if she could walk the bull. It is a quiet, reliable animal, as safe as houses, Sir, I can assure you.'

Lionel retorted, 'No bull is safe, you risked her life. I'm getting in touch with the local paper about their report, bringing my name into the story just for villagers to gossip about.'

Colin took a deep breath as he put the phone down, saying to Heather, 'We've done it now!'

Heather threw her arms around him, exclaiming as she did, 'We are in it together. Does that reassure you? Together I said.' And Colin did indeed find comfort in those words. Mrs Gilder appeared, knocking at the door, carrying two cups of tea.

'Don't worry,' she said. 'Everything's going to be all right. Nothing is straightforward in farming, or in love.' She knew, she understood.

CHAPTER TWENTY-FOUR

NEW MACHINES FOR OLD

At the Wren's Nest the weekend after the Show Colin started mowing a temporary ley. The weather had flattened the heavy crop of rye grass and clover. The old Ferguson tractor just about coped with the swath as he mowed it one way. It was a slow process. He drove his tractor and mower up the field with the machine out of gear. Then he dropped the mower with the fingers down into the crop and his tractor coughed and misfired. Although desperate to finish before the rain came, Colin conceded defeat and when Heather arrived he was sitting dejected in the kitchen.

She sized up the situation in the hay field, barely a quarter of which had been mown. Turning to the man she loved, she told him something he already knew but would not admit. 'The tractor is worn out and the trailer mower is pretty archaic. You should replace them. Sell the bull, darling, and the money could buy both.'

Colin replied, 'I know that, but when I do sell the bull that money will be for our honeymoon.'

Heather said, puckishly, 'You know you sound like a little boy, and I feel that I could roll you in the mowing grass and we'd have a romp together. But there's work to be done and I'm in this with you. I'll help you. Let's think of the future, of figures . . . and not the sort of figures you young men imagine, but money.'

The kitchen was cosy, the last rays of light faded and the mowing was abandoned for the day. Heather continued her thoughts. 'There's no need to keep that boy working for you. I'll work here every hour that's free from college. I've a jolly good mind to leave Hartbury altogether to come and work for you. You do need me.'

Still feeling down about the haymaking, Colin replied, 'That's sweet of you but for God's sake don't upset your dad any more. I'm in pretty bad odour with him already.'

Heather's mind was working on a scheme to help the lovable farmer. Finally, she came out with her idea. 'You know that firm in Gloucester that sent you a brochure of their new Ferguson tractor and an offer to test drive it. Ring them in the morning and ask them to bring their new model and rotary mower. The students at college have no trouble with it. It's quite a breakthrough.'

But Colin was not enthusiastic. 'What do I do for money? Tractors are expensive. I'll buy a second-hand one.'

Heather insisted, 'No! Buy a *new* one. The agents offer good terms, with instalments over three years.'

Colin smiled at last; so there did seem to be a way, a solution. 'My inspiration,' he said. 'Would you sit on a poor disillusioned young farmer's knee? I've something to tell you.'

Heather replied. 'I know you love me dearly, that goes without saying. You smell of tractor fuel and the cowshed, but all right then.'

After a kiss and a cuddle Colin whispered in Heather's ear, 'All right. I'll do as you suggest, but why have I more faith in a girl not yet eighteen than I have in my bank manager?'

She laughed, saying, 'Maybe it's the stockbroker instinct coming out of me from Dad.'

When the dealer brought the Massey Ferguson diesel tractor and a mower on a low loader to the farm on Monday morning three-quarters of the field was still uncut. The tractor mechanic set up the tractor and mounted mower in the hay field. Heather stood by Colin; they both watched the mechanic drive the tractor with the mounted rotary mower around the field, cutting the weather-flattened grass with ease. Heather spoke first. 'Just look at that, Colin. The machine is literally shaving the ground, leaving so little stubble, getting more hay for your cows.'

'It's doing a super job,' Colin said as he stood on the headland and compared it with the work done by the old tractor mower.

The tractor salesman had been selling tractors for many years and had every confidence in the outfit he was offering.

'Oh, yes,' he agreed. 'Your old mower wasn't too far removed from the horse-drawn machines of a hundred years ago. The agitating blade which cut the grass through the fingers has been good in its time, but you will find a mounted mower on the hydraulic lift will do a much better job, and, of course, the mower is the rotary type.'

Colin was impressed, but still hesitated. 'I don't know. I've always muddled along through haymaking with unreliable implements. It stems from Dad of course, he never bought anything new.'

'You drive it, Mr Gilder. You can drive much faster with a rotary machine; it deals with the laid crop as you can see. I expect you've noticed, mowing with your machine, that when the wind blows the grass in front of the blade you finish with a long stubble.'

As the young farmer circled the field there was no doubt in his mind that he needed the new equipment, and needed it badly. This mower left a tidy swath. He started working out figures in his head; how much would it all cost, and how much would the salesman give for his old implements? Heather, anxious to ride the new outfit herself, told Colin that she would carry on mowing while he went into the house to do business with the salesman. The figure he offered seemed fair to Colin and the old tractor was taken in part exchange. 'As for the mower, Mr Gilder, that's scrap. I'd get the scrap-iron Jacks to pick it up if I were you.'

All this time Heather was circling the field like a marathon runner, apart from the fact that each circle made the distance a little shorter. She called to the two men and Colin signalled that he had made the deal. 'Go and milk the cows,' she shouted over the throb of the diesel engine. 'I'll go on with the mowing.'

When the milking was done Colin returned to the hay field to find it almost finished. As Heather mowed the last few swaths she worked with the headlights full on, and Colin heard her singing. What a girl! He was just wondering how long he would have taken with the old equipment when Heather, now up on the headland,

called, 'How about that! It's because I love you so much I want you to get out of the rut. You know – be progressive.'

In the gathering darkness the couple linked arms as they went to the edge of the field near the brook. 'We're both tired. Shall we rest here? It's where I mowed a part of the field on Saturday, and this hay is almost made.' Colin made a haycock alongside the brook. Heather took the hint as they collapsed on the ready-made bed.

'Oh,' she sighed, a happy sigh on a soft bed in the hay. 'This is romantic and so special. Oh, Colin,' she whispered, 'Oh Colin, you can undo my shirt if you like, but no more! We're keeping our promise you know.'

Colin held his girl tightly and cried, 'Oh when, Oh when can I put a diamond ring on your finger and claim you as mine?'

'When I am eighteen, that's soon you know. You can speak then to Dad of our plans.' Teasingly she added, 'Are you really scared of him, Colin?'

He replied, 'No, my love. With you as a fantastic partner you just give me all the courage I need. We are together in this, you know.'

Heather looked at her watch. 'It's very late, Colin. I believe I've been to sleep in your arms. That's lovely! I must get home now, it's been a busy day. Happy, Colin?'

'Indescribably happy, Heather.'

On the way back to the Wren's Nest the couple looked into one of the loose boxes at the farm. One of Colin's cows was calving, and they watched the birth of the bull calf by one of the best sires in the herd book. 'Wonderful!' Heather uttered as she left in her car.

'Mind how you drive, darling. You are precious to me.' Those final words from Colin sent her on her way the few miles back to Hawthorn Farm. But Colin stayed in the yard, proud of his new calf, thinking that in ten months the sale of such a bull would help to pay for the new tractor.

How long Colin stayed there that evening, hurricane lantern in his hand, he didn't know. The time went so quickly. His mind was in top gear, his thoughts of his life with Heather and how she had advised him, of what an old head she had on such young shoulders, shoulders he just loved to hold. He dreamed on, until suddenly he remembered the tractor. 'Oh. I must get it into the barn. It's still where Heather finished the mowing.' He walked from the buildings to the new tractor, started the engine and switched on the headlights. 'This is a different world,' he thought. Compared with the old implements the knock, knock, knock of the new diesel signified power in the engine. A few more days of sunshine and the contractor could bale the winter fodder.

After the baling Heather took two more days off from college, to swot for exams and to help with the haymaking. This twentieth-century Boadicea stood aloft on the trailer, while Colin and his uncle pitched the bales for her to load. It was a tidy haymaking at the Wren's Nest that summer, the hay being required in good fettle, and Colin hoped he had turned the corner. He tried to keep his mind on the farming, but really he lived in a dream world, counting the days until he could pop the question, a question to which he already knew the answer.

The next evening Heather's studies were interrupted by a phone call from Colin. It sounded urgent. 'Can you come over tonight, darling? I must see you. I know you have exams tomorrow and should be revising, but please Heather, do come, I do so need you. You'll know it's important when you arrive.'

Heather asked, 'What ever is the matter, have I said something I shouldn't?'

Colin replied, 'Of course not. I just need you.'

When Heather arrived at the Wren's Nest Mrs Gilder met her in the yard and told her that the bull calf was dead, and the only person Colin wanted to see was Heather. 'He's in the Cider House and I'm afraid he's had too much to drink. It's understandable, poor boy. He had such high hopes for that calf.'

Heather called, 'Colin?'

Colin answered, 'I'm here, a bit delicate.'

She found him propped up against an empty barrel with tears streaming down his face. The dead calf was lying on the straw in the loose box. 'Come on now. It's not the end of the world, young farmer. You come with me.'

They sat together on bales of straw with their arms around each other. 'Steady on, Colin. Your tears are soaking my shirt, you drunken hound, but I love you more than ever.'

'It's weak of a man to cry though, Heather. And the cider hasn't drowned my sorrow. Only one thing will do that, my darling sweetheart.' Colin's voice was muted, and Heather knew he was hurt badly.

'Oh Colin. I didn't mean you were a drunkard, but you're so funny when you're under the weather. Come on into the house. I'll make you some black coffee, and we are not going to brood about this disaster.' Colin nodded. 'Then we're going out into the fresh air of the tower on the Hill. I'll drive, you're not fit, full of "Agricultural Brandy", as George would call it. You're not going to mope about here and get morbid. You know another of George's sayings: "Them as keeps hosses must expect to have losses".'

The tower, stately, elegant, a feature of eighteenth-century architecture on the brow of the Hill, was as ever a magic place for the couple. Colin sobered up after a while but tonight no moon shone to illuminate the Vale below, just stars, millions of stars. A seat below the tower made what some call a trysting place, where man and woman meet and share their joys, their sorrows. This was not the time for lovemaking, but to share that togetherness they both longed for. A time of tranquillity that acts better than medicine to the soul.

Heather laughed. Still a bit befuddled, Colin said, 'You're not laughing at me, my sweet?'

'No,' Heather replied. 'I was thinking of the MP, Conservative mind, for Evesholme, who Daddy was friendly with in his London Club. He used to say how his heart missed a beat as he drove down these hills and saw the Vale below, his constituency, in spring time with the plum trees all white with blossom. I understand him, Colin, but I must admit my heart beats faster when I'm with you.'

Some folk talk their heads off when they've had one too many; Colin was quiet, contemplative, but perked up as he listened to Heather. 'Did you hear what I said, Colin, when I said about the magic of this place. Some sites are like the standing stones, steeped in the mystery of our ancestors. They really are special.'

'Oh, damn the calf! I'm not at my best tonight, Heather. Do forgive me, please.'

Heather replied, 'There's nothing to forgive. I'm trying to share the trouble with you.'

Colin was very thoughtful and, with his arm around her shoulder he sighed, a happy sigh. 'Do I really deserve such a treasure, because I think you are just that.'

'I'll soon be eighteen and you know what I promised you then.'

Colin assured her that that was always in his thoughts. 'But now you must take me home, and you must return to Hawthorn Farm.'

In the lounge at Hawthorn Farm Lionel and Pamela were having their usual nightcap. Lionel was apparently in one of his better moods when Heather arrived. 'Fancy a drink, Heather?'

She agreed to have a sherry. Pamela didn't seem to share Lionel's mood and complained about her staying out late rather than revising. 'You must put first things first, Heather, because it's so important if you are to get a place at Reading University.'

Heather burst out crying, and Pamela was bemused. 'Now what have I said?'

Heather replied, 'It's nothing you've said, but Colin's special bull calf has died from what's known as white scour or dysentery.'

Lionel's response was predictable. 'That's surely neglect. I gather it's common to immunise against that today.'

Heather snapped, 'Dad, he did. You can't accuse him of neglect. He's a good stockman, so particular as farmers go.'

Lionel replied, 'But farmers, and Colin, must expect losses today. Prices are down, land values have fallen. Our insurance companies no longer buy land for investment. There's no future in farming, particularly dairy farming. People don't drink so much milk nowadays. Farmers have turned more to growing oil seed rape for cooking oils, but they'll overdo that too.'

Heather, still upset over Colin's calf, tried to make sense of her father's speech. 'Oh, Dad. Farming has gone through bad patches before. I'm wondering whether we did the right thing joining the Common Market and letting down the Commonwealth, but you know that Ministry chap at your Club in Cheltenham, he's a "Job's Comforter" if ever there was one. I don't want to work for his sort at the Ministry of Agriculture. You say he's retiring, not before time! Give me dairy farming and lambing pens.'

Pamela, backing up her husband on his ill-informed ideas, said, 'Your dad is right. For some time now the writing's been on the wall for farmers, and the Ministry *is* the place to work. One meets the nicest people there, a good class of intelligent folk. I just don't know what the farmers would do without the Advisory Service. Oh, farmers are so parochial, when they plant their crops, rear their livestock, they haven't a clue what the public requires. There's a growing demand for organic food today but few will change their policy. They keep soaking the land with chemicals.'

Heather retorted, 'That's just the point! It's a matter of someone, or some body of folk, making a move towards better farming practice. For instance, if farmers were encouraged by the "Long-haired Intellectuals" to go back to the time when crops were grown in rotation, and some land fallowed every year, there would be less need for chemicals. I think the Young Farmers have more sense than some of the Ministry lot. Oh, good night! I'm off to bed.'

CHAPTER TWENTY-FIVE

THE EIGHTEENTH
BIRTHDAY PARTY

Colin and Heather had decided a little while ago that they would get engaged when Heather was eighteen. Their joy was blighted somewhat by thoughts of Lionel's reaction. Even though at eighteen Heather could please herself, she felt that for her Dad to agree, however grudgingly, would be much better. Lionel and Pamela had arranged a party for Heather. The whole family, their son, Charles, and their other daughter, Barbara, with her husband, Jeremy, were all to come. Pamela commented, 'We must invite Colin or we'll never be forgiven.'

Lionel gave one of his disapproving grunts and said, 'I suppose so. One day she may see sense and not waste her life with a chap with no breeding.'

Pamela, with a sigh, tried to say something in the young farmer's favour. 'But darling, he's awfully good looking.'

Gwyn and Nesta Williams came with Fiona. Despite his low opinion of farmers, Lionel did like Gwyn. At least he'd been to Cirencester Agricultural College, and he'd been very good in his advice on buying the pony. Gwyn knew that Colin was going to ask Lionel's approval for his intention to marry his daughter. He whispered to the young man at the party, 'Take the bull by the horns, ask him now.'

Heather whispered back, 'Don't mention bulls!' She was not enjoying the party but knew that she and Colin were sitting on what amounted to a time-bomb, which would explode when Lionel was asked for his blessing.

Revd Philip Lamb proposed a toast to Heather. His words didn't exactly please Lionel:

Here's health and happiness to you Heather on your eighteenth birthday. A wonderful future I am sure lies ahead of you. Whatever that future is, it is in God's hands. If it is farming, I'm sure you will be a success. It's a wonderful career, producing the food for our tables season after season. Be upstanding. To Heather, Many Happy Returns of the Day!

Looking redfaced after several whiskies, Lionel said aside to his wife, 'What a lot of blather. He needn't have said that about farming. I've told him our desire is for Heather to get an executive post in the Ministry of Agriculture. If she goes farming with young Gilder it means being tied to a cow's tail for life. I've seen it happen so often, the women bear the brunt of it all. Oh, the filth of a cow pen and the lambing, it doesn't bear thinking about. It's all very well Philip Lamb talking like that, his son is going into a proper profession – the Church.'

Pamela interrupted, 'Not so loud, Lionel, we don't want to upset the Rector. Have another drink, it should be a happy day for us all.'

As the party ended Heather and Colin were talking to Fiona and Charles in the lounge. Heather whispered to Colin, 'Dad's in the library, could you speak to him now?'

Colin replied nervously, 'Okay. You ask him if it is convenient. Keep your fingers crossed!'

Heather encouraged him, 'It's okay, Colin. You know how much I love you. Don't be afraid of Dad.'

As Colin walked quickly into the library he rehearsed his words one last time. 'Can I have a word with you, Sir?'

Lionel replied sharply, 'What do you want, boy? The guests have all gone, it's time you were gone. I always thought that farmers were early birds and early to rest.'

Colin stammered, 'Erm . . . er . . .'.

Lionel retorted, 'Come on lad, say what you have to say. I'm just off to bed.'

Colin blurted out, 'Heather and I want to get engaged. I thought I should get your approval.'

Lionel snapped, 'The answer is No. She's too young to know her own mind, not to make the mistake of being tied to a cow's tail.'

Colin replied, 'We do love each other, that's important, isn't it?'

Lionel growled, 'Yes, but what are her prospects? She should finish her education and see a bit more of the world than these hills and the peasants who live here.'

Colin replied glumly, 'Good night, Sir. She *is* eighteen and must make up her own mind.'

Meeting Heather in the hall Colin told her what Lionel's answer was – a foregone conclusion, they knew. 'Never mind, darling Colin. We love each other. You were brave to tackle Dad like you did.'

In their bedroom Lionel, now thoroughly depressed, said, 'I wish we'd never seen Hawthorn Farm or the uncivilised country oafs round here.'

Pamela tried to comfort him. 'Don't upset yourself, think of your blood pressure.'

The next morning the dialogue between Pamela and Lionel continued. Pamela said, 'I don't think she will marry Colin. She'll meet lots of young men at the college, but then again, he is a nice lad, well mannered.'

Lionel groaned. 'What a prospect. I'll bet the bank owns his farm like the rest of the farmers, it'll be mortgaged up to the hilt. I've said no to his proposal but Heather has agreed.'

Heather told her father that at eighteen she could please herself. 'He was just being polite, Dad.'

'I'll make a bargain with you, Heather,' he responded. 'If you'll delay the engagement for a year I'll buy you a Morgan sports car. I know Morgans of Malvern, they make quality stuff, only manufacture a few cars a month.'

Heather replied with prim patience, 'That's jolly good of you Dad, but no. We are getting engaged.'

As Heather drove off to college Lionel phoned Phil Grafton to tell him that he wouldn't be going to Town that day. Then he told

Pamela about his offer of a sports car. She agreed that it was a fair offer, but reminded him too that love is blind. 'They will get engaged on Saturday. Colin has the ring. Don't you think we should invite him over, and his mother, for a drink?'

'Oh, very well then, please yourself,' Lionel snapped. 'But I'm not condoning it. I suppose no harm will be done.'

As the two families met later at Hawthorn Farm, pleasantries were exchanged and Pamela tried her best to be friendly with Mrs Gilder. She inquired about her bed and breakfast venture at the Wren's Nest since her husband died.

Mrs Gilder too tried hard to be friendly. 'What a nice spot you have here, Mrs Bainbridge, the best of both worlds, Hill and Vale. It must be a change from London.'

But Lionel was ill at ease, his own obstinacy causing him to suffer.

A little time later Lionel mentioned that, since the engagement, young Colin had said no more of his intentions. 'It may go on for years. Engagements do, you know, then they collapse.'

Pamela chided him. 'They're in love and biding their time. They're as good as married now.'

Lionel gasped, 'What on earth do you mean? You're not suggesting that they're cohabiting!'

Pamela replied, 'Things are very different from when you and I were engaged. Society is more liberal.'

Lionel was now despondent. 'We waited until the wedding night. It seems there's no restraint today.'

Colin and Heather had decided they would marry when Heather was nineteen. Once more Colin came to confront Lionel. He explained their decision and finished by asking, 'I hope you will give us your blessing, Sir.'

Lionel snapped, 'I've said before, and I say it again, my daughter is too young to make up her mind. Damn it man! I was twenty-nine when we married. Young folk rush into marriage too quickly. It *is* for life you know.'

Tentatively, Colin told him more of their plans. 'We would like a church wedding, but if not it will be at the Register Office. Do please think seriously about it, Sir. I do love your daughter.'

In the breakfast room later Pamela heard Lionel crying bitterly. She put her arm round his shoulder and said, 'Oh, darling. What's the matter? Have you had a row with Colin? Don't let it upset you like this.'

Lionel replied, still sobbing, 'No, Pamela, there's been no row. But Colin is determined to steal our daughter. We've lost her now.'

Pamela tried to comfort him. 'You shouldn't say that. Colin loves her very much. He's a worker at least, I do like that.'

CHAPTER TWENTY-SIX

HAPPY LETTERS

When Heather returned to college at Hartbury she had mixed feelings. She loved Colin to distraction, but it hurt to see her father so determined to stop their wedding. 'I'll write to Colin and try to explain my feelings,' she thought.

Monday

My Dearest Colin

You are a lovely spirit and you are my love. This is to tell you that we will go to the forest again one day, and that your heart can always come home to me. Remember the crescent moon that night as we flew home through the lanes?

This morning I woke early, with such a sudden start. I thought you were talking to me. I heard your voice right next to me, very clear. When I looked around there was only the sun coming up through the leafy trees and over the hill. I picture you at the Young Farmers. Oh, they all love you, but not a thousandth part as much as I do.

Heather

Tuesday

My Darling Colin

Oh dear, I did so think that you would ring me this morning, but I tell myself you must be busy with the farm, which makes me happy again. I woke very early again this morning. It was all so pearly and beautiful. I felt I was out there high up in the great powdery elm trees with the birds and the clouds. I sent it all to you, darling, in my spirit. Did you get it?

You said yesterday that I sometimes seem to have tears in my eyes, but if I am with you they must be tears of love not of sorrow. You understand so many of the lovely things that catch at me and bring tears to my eyes. Beauty sometimes does it, when one is living from the heart, and you channel these things right through, and give them back to everyone else. That's more than enough to bring tears to my eyes, and it's so lovely to know I can put my head on your shoulder and cry that happiness out of love. I don't make much sense, do I? I know you will understand. You are my solace, my strength, my sweetness. Before I met you I was half dead, but now my heart is coming to life again, and my spirit is returning home like a bird. You have given these things back to me so I keep them for you. I hope that you ring me tonight.

Sleep well, I do love you, you know.

Heather

Colin rang to tell her that her letters gave him such confidence in the future, that they softened the blow that Lionel had dealt him, and that he too remembered the time they spent in the Forest of Dean, and on Bredon Hill. After speaking with him, Heather decided to send another letter.

Friday

Dearest Colin,

Such a day of peace and happiness. I wish you could know the feeling of loveliness that is flooding through me this morning, but perhaps you are feeling it too. It is because now I know your heart; before I knew your spirit and your mind, but sharing the painful moments has opened the door of your heart to me.

Our day in the Forest was magical and whatever the mystery of love is, it was with us for all that day. You couldn't have made me happier. I will *never* forget that day. The Forest seemed to take us into its spirit. I finally began to know your heart and all its depth. Thank you, thank you. Do you know, I'm listening to Elgar as I write this, and thinking of our drive beside the Malverns under those troubled English skies.

I love you.

Heather

Heather was unable to see Colin for a while. She was busy with her studies and he felt so unwelcome at Hawthorn Farm. In fact, Lionel said if he came he must stay on the driveway. Heather rang the one she loved as often as she could, and got great pleasure too in expressing her feelings to him in letters. In one she wrote of their day on Bredon Hill and the Folly on the summit, of the richness of the natural beauty that had surrounded them, of how being there together seemed to release them from their worries, and of how she looked forward to their wedding day. Heather was so moved that her feelings overflowed into verse:

> Being together . . .
> Looking down on our life together,
> Looping river, coloured fields.
> All those who are still here, though dead, around us.
> And the sound of Saturday bells, from a village below,
> Ringing out for a wedding, not knowing it was ours.

This still holds. It is a wedding of the spirit.

Much Love,

Heather. xx

CHAPTER TWENTY-SEVEN

UNHAPPY EVENTS

After writing her letters to Colin, Heather felt that the cold shoulder that her father had given to the man she loved so dearly could test his relationship with her. Coming back to Hawthorn Farm she found Lionel in a bad way, in the slough of despond, as she called it.

Lionel was not at the office. Phil, the chauffeur, had been told that his boss had a heavy cold, but when it persisted for days, he began to wonder. Lionel rested in bed. Taking his breakfast and the morning paper to the bedroom, Pamela asked if he was feeling a little better.

Lionel snapped, 'Of course I'm not. This is a blow below the belt.'

Pamela was very concerned and couldn't decide whether she should send for the Doctor or the Rector. She settled for Philip Lamb, the Rector. 'Oh, Philip,' she began. 'Could you come over and see Lionel. He's not at all well. It's over Heather's proposed wedding, you know. He's beside himself with worry.'

'I'll be along shortly, Pamela, of course. I'll bring him a bottle of my home-made wine to cheer him up a bit.'

Pamela thought, 'He will be lucky.' She knew her husband when he was in a black mood.

Revd Lamb knew how difficult the situation would be. Whatever he said to Lionel would be wrong. His opening words did not impress. 'I'm sorry to see you under the weather. I do understand your concern over your daughter, but those on the sidelines can often see more of the play you know, and I think that you're fortunate that Heather will be marrying Colin.'

Lionel sat up in bed, took another slurp of his whisky from the glass on the side table, and bellowed, 'What! A common farmer, a peasant with no education. No, it's a *tragedy* that she should marry a man who is so much lower on the social scale.'

Philip tried his best. 'Suppose your daughter was engaged to a drug addict, or an alcoholic, that wouldn't please you, even if he was a stockbroker.'

Lionel retorted, 'If that's all the comfort you have for me you had better go, and take your rhubarb wine. I'm in no mood to listen to sermons. Leave me, please.'

Downstairs, Revd Lamb and Pamela were concerned, of course, but couldn't help laughing. As the Rector explained, 'Sorry, Pamela. I didn't cut much ice with him.'

'I knew you wouldn't, but at least you tried,' Pamela consoled him.

'He's in a bad way, Pamela. I'll pray for him, but don't tell him for that would incense him, you know. Frankly, Pamela, I'd get the Doctor. He needs medication. Maybe a course of tranquillisers would help him over the hurdle, and believe me it is a hurdle . . . and a trial for you too. I am sorry.'

The following day Lionel's doctor, a cheerful, middle-aged Scot, arrived from Cheltenham. Lionel told the old story about his ambitions for his daughter Heather to work for the EEC in Brussels but how she had chosen to marry a dog-and-stick farmer who grew nothing but grass and milked seventy cows.

The Doctor answered him cautiously, 'I'm sure things will turn out for the best, they usually do. But the saying goes "If she makes her bed, she must lie on it".' He thought a while and, knowing his patient was not short of money, in fact, that was an understatement, he suggested, 'Why don't you and Pamela go away for a holiday? You both need a change.'

Lionel sat up in bed, raising his voice. 'What! Leave our daughter to be vamped by the young farmers around. I don't like their coarseness. They raise animals and behave like them. It's all written on the windscreens of their Land Rovers – "Young farmers do it in their wellies!" Pretty disgusting, don't you think?'

The Doctor laughed. 'Come on, Lionel. Young folk have a different sense of humour than you or I have. I'm going to put you on some tranquillisers. That'll get rid of your stress and help you to sleep.'

Lionel snapped, 'Valium I suppose. Make me into a zombie. I want to keep aware of the situation.'

The Doctor said, 'They're not addictive. I'll send you medium strength, 5 milligrams. I do advise you to keep off whisky, the tablets don't mix with spirits.'

Lionel gasped, 'Damn it, Doctor. You take away the only pleasure left now sex is out of the question.'

As the Doctor said goodbye to his patient he added, 'Take the tablets and stop worrying.'

When the tablets arrived Lionel flushed them down the lavatory and continued to dope himself with whisky. The Doctor failed to convince him that whisky was a drug and that tranquillisers were much better for him. The suggestion that Lionel should see a psychiatrist really roused him. 'What! Like the flaming Yanks, they all have their trick cyclists these days, putting everything down to sex or the lack of it. I don't trust them, Doctor.'

'Give the medicine a chance, Lionel,' the Doctor pleaded, adding, 'It's no good if you don't trust us or the medicine.'

After the Doctor left Pamela begged her husband to accept Heather's decision to marry Colin. Lionel was adamant. 'Do not let that chap into our house.'

'That will make him feel unwelcome! I shall ask him into the hall. He's a jolly nice lad. I'm getting to like him.

There followed a couple of days of misery, with Lionel getting up in the afternoon, drinking and sleeping. Another visit from the Doctor proved fruitless, as Lionel had refused the tablets. After the medical man had left, Lionel dressed himself and told Pamela he was going for a walk. In fact, he walked to the Pear Tree Inn and drank yet more whisky. Sam the landlord brought Lionel home at closing time. Pamela had been so worried, but Lionel told her that he'd met a colonel there, who must be ninety, who had served in India and now lived in Cheltenham, and that they'd got chatting.

The next day Heather told her dad that there was no need for him to walk to the Pear Tree. 'You have Phil, and I could take you and fetch you back if you want to meet the Colonel. You pay Phil, use him Daddy. We worry about you wandering about.'

At that point, Revd Lamb came breezing into the room. 'Hello, Lionel. What's this I hear about you wandering off to the Pear Tree? I know just how you feel. I'd like to run away sometimes and behave like a teenager, but do look after yourself. God loves you, you know.'

Lionel was not comforted in the least. 'If He loves me, He's the only one who does,' he grunted.

Philip Lamb was an experienced country parson. He had helped sort out marriage problems and had worked with the youngsters at the youth club. He was used to difficult situations, and it certainly seemed as if here was another one. The stubborn stockbroker was insisting on going alone to drink at the inn, making excuses about advising the Colonel on some shares. Philip tried again to dissuade him. 'I'll take you, Lionel. It's no trouble,' he offered as he left Hawthorn Farm. But Lionel insisted that the walk would do him good.

At the Pear Tree that evening the Colonel's daughter called for her father and offered Lionel a lift in her car. 'Damn it, that's good of you, but on a night like this with the moon at full the walk will be good for me. All I get at home from Pamela is "You should take the valium, dear", so I don't want to get back too soon.'

As this new countryman who had escaped from city life took the bridle path towards home through the woods, relaxed by the whisky but a little unsteady on his feet, the tawny owl hooted and the odd badger or two crossed the rides between the trees. Lionel thought he should turn along this footpath, but although the moon showed a well-worn track he managed to miss the stile and wandered through the hazel undergrowth until his progress was halted by a barbed wire fence.

CHAPTER TWENTY-EIGHT

ON THE WIRE

'Damn these farmers,' Lionel said to himself, 'blocking up footpaths, riding roughshod over the countryside. It's no wonder the Ramblers Association is continually at loggerheads with them.' He glared at the barbed wire fence. 'A scourge of the land,' he thought. 'I'll double my subscription to the Ramblers Association. But surely I can manage this fence.'

As he tried to climb over the fence in his befuddled state, Lionel slipped and fell; his clothes caught on the barbed wire leaving him hanging helplessly on the fence, balanced precariously with one foot just touching a tree stump. He was unable to move. The owl hooted, the wind increased, the air was chill, and the hoar-frost was already sparkling in the moonlight on the bramble bushes.

Half an hour after closing time at the Pear Tree Pamela rang the landlord, worried because Lionel had not returned. Still in her dressing gown, she rushed in desperation to Phil's flat begging him to go to George's cottage as Lionel might be there drinking as he had on a previous occasion.

George called from his bedroom window, 'No, Phil, I haven't seen the Gaffer all day.'

Heather phoned Colin and told him her father had been missing for hours, and would he please come quickly. Telling her to stay by the phone, Colin dressed quickly and made for Hawthorn Farm in his Land Rover. He then drove along one of the bridle paths towards Blossomfield and the Pear Tree. 'Thank God it's moonlight,' he thought, as through the woods the moon gave some light in the clearings among the trees. But when the woods closed in, it was completely dark beyond the headlights of the vehicle.

At a junction of the rides Colin stopped his vehicle. Taking a torch from the shelf in front of his steering wheel, he got out and listened. The tawny owl was noisy that night, and normally Colin loved to listen to it calling, but not tonight – he was listening for a possible cry for help. Faintly, that call came. 'Help. Help. Help.'

Colin called back, 'I'm coming. Where are you?'

The answer came, 'Come quickly. I can't get away', and the beam of Colin's torch picked out a man in tweeds hanging on a fence. Colin rushed towards what he saw and was horrified. Lionel Bainbridge was hanging there by his clothes from a barbed wire fence, the whole weight of his body supported only by one foot on a tree stump.

Colin told Lionel not to struggle and to put his arm around his shoulder. Lionel said that no sooner had he released himself from the barbs than he became caught up again. His hands and legs were bleeding. Soon Colin had released him from the wire. 'There you are, Sir. You're free. Just sit down under that tree and I'll bring the Land Rover nearer.'

Speaking like a medic, Colin reassured Lionel, who, shocked as he was, even so replied, 'I can walk to the Land Rover if you help me, boy. Don't leave me.'

Colin was anxious to get Lionel away, and said, 'Now, take it steady. Just put your arm around my shoulders. This way.' The two men stumbled along to the Land Rover.

As soon as Colin arrived at Blossomfield he phoned Heather from the kiosk there to tell her that he was taking her father to the casualty department at Cheltenham Hospital. 'Oh, you darling!' was Heather's reply. 'I'll meet you at the hospital with Mother. Is Dad all right? Not too bad? See you soon.'

Back at the Land Rover Lionel was a changed man. He realised that Colin had saved his life, and said so too. 'I couldn't have held on much longer you know.' Colin was anxious to get his patient to casualty but listened intently to the stockbroker. 'I'll never forget this. Why did you bother? I've never done anything for you.'

Colin replied as they entered the town, 'That's all right, Sir. We will soon be at the hospital. Are you cold?'

'Yes, I am. I could do with some more whisky.'

Colin, who had done a course with the St John Ambulance Brigade, told Lionel, 'If you have hypothermia the hospital staff will warm you with an electric blanket. Whisky gives a warm glow but does nothing to warm the body.'

At the hospital Heather and her mother were waiting on the steps. Pamela burst into tears when she saw the blood on Lionel's shirt and cried, 'Oh my God! Lionel, what have you done?'

In a quiet voice Lionel replied, 'This boy has saved my life.' Pamela threw her arms around Lionel, then around Colin as her husband went into casualty.

The usual routine of tetanus injections followed, and the doctor gave instructions for Lionel to be treated for hypothermia. In the small hours, after ensuring that everything would be all right, Colin drove Heather back to Hawthorn Farm. Pamela stayed on the ward with her husband, who told her over and over how Colin had rescued him. 'My word, Pamela, he's as strong as an ox. He almost carried me through the wood.'

Pamela looked her husband straight in the face as he lay propped up in bed. 'Yes, he's a good man. I'm sure he's good for Heather. Be nice to him now. He's going to be one of the family.'

Lionel replied quietly, 'I'll think about it, but I'm in no fit state to make decisions at the moment. Mind you, I'm truly grateful to Colin. He's restored my faith in human nature.'

The Bainbridge's other daughter, Barbara, arrived early in the morning from London, driving, as she said, 'Up the M40 and the A40 like a bat out of hell.' She had a good bedside manner, her husband, Jeremy was a surgeon. Whether Lionel was happy to hear her comments is doubtful, but the words had to be said. 'You know, Daddy, I do think Heather's so lucky to have a chap like Colin at her side. Jeremy is a sweety but to be honest, I'm a teeny weeny bit jealous! Anyway Dad, I'm glad to see you safe and being cared for.'

Lionel leant over to the bedside table and said, 'Take this bottle of whisky to Colin with my regards.'

After dropping Heather at Hawthorn Farm, Colin had gone home to the Wren's Nest, but not before he had impressed on her that he wanted to have a talk with her father as soon as possible. On the phone later that day she told him that she could detect more than a slight softening in Lionel's attitude regarding the wedding. 'You know, Dad has really taken a shine towards you, and you know how I feel. I know that what you did for Dad, you would have done for anyone.'

It was 5 o'clock in the afternoon when Colin visited Lionel. He entered the ward smartly dressed in a pair of new cord trousers, a check shirt and a sweater to match. Lionel began straightaway. 'Well, boy, you can see I'm still alive. There's a lot of folk in the churchyard who'd be glad of my scars. Have you milked yet? I don't want you to neglect the farm because of me. I'll be here a few days yet, but it's good to see you.'

'Good to see you! Well, that's something,' Colin thought to himself. 'I milked at 3 o'clock this afternoon, a bit early,' he replied.

Lionel had always been a generous chap to those he took to, but never before to Colin. He wondered how he could give this young farmer just a token of his respect. 'You know that garage near the Pear Tree where I get my petrol? Fill up your Land Rover and put it on my account.'

Colin replied, 'Thank you, Sir, but it's a diesel.'

'Well, fill up with diesel, I know these Land Rovers are a bit thirsty.' Lionel wanted to say things to Colin but without appearing to climb down. 'How's your Mother?' He thought perhaps that would break the ice.

'She's very well, busy, of course, with the bed and breakfast.'

After an awkward pause Colin heard the words he had waited for. 'I . . . I don't object any longer to your marrying my daughter Heather – on certain conditions.' The clause 'on certain conditions' was really a little way Lionel had devised to avoid what might appear to be a complete turn around. He was, after all, a hard-headed businessman.

'What conditions, Sir?' Colin asked with some anxiety.

'Where's your mother going to live, for as good a woman as she is, it's not wise for you and Heather to live with her. We'll think of something. She must stay in the farmhouse and do her bed and breakfast. You know the old adage, Colin?'

'No, Sir, I don't understand what you mean.'

Lionel's dry sense of humour, seldom understood, still had a spark or two left. He recited:

> 'Two cats and one mouse,
> Two dogs and one bone,
> Two women in one house,
> Will never agree long.'

That said it all; Lionel was thinking of something.

Colin left for the Wren's Nest where Heather was waiting with Mrs Gilder. They were drinking tea in the sitting-room when he rushed breathless into the house. 'I've seen your Dad and he's got no objections to our wedding!'

Heather gasped. 'That's great! I felt it all along in my bones.' And she threw her arms around him.

Mrs Gilder left the lovers, making the excuse that she had things to do in the kitchen. She was in bed, much later, when she finally heard Colin and Heather in the yard saying their good nights. Heather, homeward bound for Hawthorn Farm, fairly purred like a contented cat as the car sped through the night. No one, but no one would chastise her for being late. At last, this young spirit would no longer be treated as a child.

CHAPTER TWENTY-NINE

THE HEIFERS

At college the following day Heather felt liberated knowing that, at long last, her father had accepted Colin, but those conditions still lingered in her mind. What conditions had her father got in mind? Colin hadn't told her all of it. She was willing to live in a cottage, but knew that her father would not approve. The couple longed to find out just what Lionel was planning.

When Heather rang the Wren's Nest in the evening Colin sounded a bit down. She sensed something was wrong. 'Darling,' she said softly, 'you don't sound yourself. I hope it's nothing I've said or done, do tell me, please.'

Colin replied, 'I've had a letter this morning. The bank isn't prepared to give me a loan. It means, bluntly, that I'm unable to expand the herd unless I can get some money from somewhere else, and the twenty young heifers I have reared will have to be sold. They are all in calf and it breaks my heart to sell them. Increase production the Ministry said in the past; now it's cutting back.'

Heather, trying to be constructive, replied, 'Oh, I'll sell my car, I'll sell Bronwyn my pony, my Premium Bonds . . .'.

'No, you mustn't,' Colin interrupted, but at the same time loving the spirit of the girl. 'It's my fault for rearing the heifers.'

After a week in hospital, Lionel returned to Hawthorn Farm. When he called at the surgery his GP was pleased with his recovery, but suggested that he cut down on his drinking, and that the sooner he got back to his office the better. 'Work's a good therapy you know.' Lionel knew that the therapy that had healed his mind was his acceptance of Colin.

Phil was glad to be back to the old routine with trips to Evesholme and helping George Burford in the garden. Pamela accompanied her husband on the train for his first week back at the office, spending her time with Barbara.

Pamela knew her husband better than he thought and realised that, in some respects, he was happier in the company of other men rather than women. Sir Francis Nabaro, the MP for the constituency, used the train from Evesholme to Paddington frequently. Pamela kept a little in the background when Sir Francis got into Lionel's carriage at the next station. They had a lot to talk about in the world of finance. After exchanging pleasantries with the MP, she would retire to the next carriage, settling down with a coffee. Sir Francis was always polite. 'Are you sure, Mrs Bainbridge? That is considerate of you, and I'm so glad to see Lionel fighting fit again.'

The Bainbridges took the 3 o'clock train home those first few days, the journey giving them a chance to discuss the wedding in three months' time.

One evening, after Heather arrived back from college, her mother found her in tears in the drawing-room of Hawthorn Farm. 'What's the trouble, darling? I hope everything's all right between you and Colin.' She dried her daughter's tears and, with soothing words, said, 'Come on now, tell me what's wrong.'

Heather sobbed. 'It couldn't be better between Colin and me. We're so looking forward to my birthday and the wedding. The trouble is Colin's finances. You know the Government is making cuts, they no longer encourage increased production. In fact, it appears that the dairy farmers have been too successful.'

Lionel entered the room and joined the conversation. 'I overheard something about finances and Colin's heifers. You know, looking back the boy has been forward-looking rearing those replacement heifers. I don't know what the world is coming to, a surplus of milk, a butter mountain and people starving.'

Heather, still sobbing, replied, 'Colin will probably have to sell the heifers at a loss. I've promised to sell my car and my pony and Premium Bonds so that he can arrange a loan from the bank.'

'Now look here my girl! Don't do anything so drastic. Send young Colin along and I'll talk to him.' A word on the phone from Lionel to his prospective son-in-law and Colin promised to come to Hawthorn Farm after he had done the milking.

As Colin finished the milking and was changing his clothes the phone rang. It was Heather, assuring him that her father was out to help them, and he should not be nervous when they met. 'I'm not nervous now, my sweet, but it's the fact that no one has helped me since Dad died. I feel a bit indebted to you and your dad.'

'Oh, forget it, dear. I love you so much and believe that Dad shows affection, and to be sure Mummy does.'

At Hawthorn Farm the set-up of drinks on a table in front of the fire, in a room where the furniture just shouted wealth, had become a ritual practised by the new countryman of Hawthorn Farm. 'Sit down, lad. What's all this trouble about your finances? I understand loans can be arranged. You know, Colin, farming is getting almost as complex as the stock market. I'll see what can be arranged.'

Colin rose from his chair and took Lionel by the hand, saying, 'Thank you, Sir. That's so kind of you. It takes a weight off my mind.' He explained that the first few heifers were due to calve in five months' time, two months after the wedding.

Fast becoming a true father figure, Lionel asked Colin if it was true that he and Heather proposed living in a cottage at the Wren's Nest. Colin said that he must live near the dairy. 'Couldn't you live in a self-contained flat, starting married life at Hawthorn Farm?' But this generous idea of Lionel's was not practical; for a dairy farmer to be a few miles from his herd was not viable.

On the Sunday morning Heather was home from college. George Burford came up the drive with a loaded wheelbarrow. He had sprouts, cooking apples, and a basket of Blenheim Orange eating apples for Pamela's kitchen. Lionel thanked the old retainer for his produce fresh from the garden. George replied, 'They tell me Heather and Colin be getting married on her birthday. I be so pleased, 'cos I reckon they be meant for one another.'

Lionel sighed. 'It seems only yesterday since Heather started school. How time passes.'

George nodded. 'I be in me seventies you know. Where be they going to live, Sir? If that ent an impertinent question.'

Lionel then told George the family was worried because the couple were going to start married life in a cottage at the Wren's Nest. 'Oh dear,' George replied. 'Oh dear. That cot ent a very good house. I minds the time when my Uncle lived there. 'Tis damp and cold.'

Master and man stood by the empty barrow after George had wheeled his produce to the kitchen door. A thought came to the old farm-hand and he wondered whether to mention it. He was always careful not to appear interfering in the affairs of his employers. After hesitating a while, he finally said, 'You know your business, Sir, but what about that holding anant Colin's farm. A good house and 20 acres of pasture. It's for sale, no doubt you know.'

Lionel gasped, 'What, George? A house next to the Wren's Nest. Colin hasn't told me.' But George knew that Colin would do no such thing because it would look as if he were hinting for Lionel to buy the property.

CHAPTER THIRTY

A New Home

The property known as The Close had apparently been on the market for some time. It belonged to a vet who kept a few horses next to Colin's cow ground. Lionel wasted no time and was soon arranging to go and see the place. He rushed back to Pamela, telling her to be ready to drive to the Wren's Nest in five minutes.

Wondering what all the hurry was, Heather asked her father, 'What's wrong?'

Lionel replied, 'Nothing's wrong. Your mother is fetching the Volvo, and we're going to see a house for sale called The Close, next to the Wren's Nest.'

Heather said, 'I know it, it's behind a little spinney, you can't see it from Colin's farm, but the fields adjoin his place.'

Lionel was in a hurry. 'Come on then. You and your mother. I want to view it now. It's a bit on the QT, mind. We don't want it to get around, not even to the Graftons.'

Mrs Gilder met them in the yard saying that Colin had a cow calving in the barn, but they must come in and have a coffee. Colin met them a few minutes later, apologising for being messy but pleased to see them. Lionel drew him to one side. 'I want a word with you. Why on earth didn't you tell me there was a property nearby for sale? It joins your fields. Heather says it's behind a spinney over there. We've come to see it.'

Colin was apologetic. 'But the price is out of our range. I think they are asking far too much, but I'll come with you and show you the place.'

He washed and changed and was soon with the Bainbridges in the car. As they drove, he explained that the house belonged to a retired

vet who had gone to live in Ireland, and he used to keep a few horses
on the 20 acres. When the party arrived at The Close, however, they
were met with the estate agent's sign which proclaimed: VIEWING
STRICTLY BY APPOINTMENT.

'Damn that for a tale!' snarled Lionel. 'I'm going to look around
the house. I know the law on trespass.'

Heather smiled at Colin. 'That's Dad all over,' she said. 'Nothing
will stop him when he makes up his mind.'

The house was built in the eighteenth century of Cotswold stone
with stone slates. The mellow outside was broken up with sash
windows and a fine oak front door. Peering through the windows,
Lionel got a good idea of the suitability of the place. A walled-in
garden was knee high in ragwort, but that presented no problems.
A small barn and stables at the back looked pretty sound and the
owner had built himself a garage by the side of the house. 'Well,
what do you think? You're the ones who will live here if I buy it,
and if it's to your liking I *shall* buy it tomorrow.'

Colin said, 'It's a great property but the asking price is high. Over
the top I should say.'

Lionel asked, 'What are they asking for it?'

Colin quietly and a bit hesitantly told him the price, to which
Lionel responded, 'Oh, they will come down on that as houses aren't
selling at the moment. It's surprising what effect it has if a cheque
book is waved in front of these agents!'

'Shouldn't you have a survey done, dear?' These cautious words
from Pamela were ignored by Lionel, who turned to Colin.

'I don't like paying huge fees to these sorts of folk. My builder
will vet this place. He knows all about woodworm and dry rot.'

Lionel was up early on the Monday morning and rang Phil to say
that he would not be going to Town, he had business to do at home.
Pamela was a bit concerned when she found Lionel making phone
calls at 7.15 a.m. 'Who are you trying to ring this early?'

Lionel replied, 'What time do builders start work these days?
I want Taylor to come and see The Close.'

Mr Taylor replied, at last. Lionel told him that he needed to see him urgently, that he would be at the estate agents at 9 o'clock to get the keys, and that he wanted Mr Taylor to give an opinion of the place. Mr Taylor knew the property, but also thought the asking price was steep. He agreed to meet Lionel and the agents at 10.30.

A junior from the agents showed Lionel, Pamela and Heather over the house with Mr Taylor, who said the house was in good shape apart from the wiring and the decorations. The windows and doors were original and very good. When the asking price was mentioned the young representative of the agents said, 'If you want to make an offer, Sir, you must talk to the senior partner. Could you come along to Cheltenham this morning and he can tell you the score.'

When Pamela dropped Lionel off at the estate agents in The Promenade he told her to book a table at the Queens Hotel for him, Pamela and Heather for 1 o'clock lunch, and advised the ladies to spend the time before then shopping.

'I'll be quite honest with you, Mr Martin,' Lionel said to the agent. 'The price is a bit steep in these times. I'll make a firm offer now.'

Mr Martin rang the owner, saying that he had a genuine buyer for The Close, who had made an offer. The owner replied that he would split the difference and Lionel agreed on condition that Mr Taylor, his builder, could start work on the house without delay.

'You hold the money, Mr Martin, and my solicitor will arrange with the vendor's solicitor over the conveyance, and so on. You see, Mr Martin, my daughter is getting married soon. We need the house quickly.'

Over lunch, Pamela and Heather had to hear the story of how Lionel had knocked down the price of The Close. No doubt the tale would be told to the Club too.

'Dad looks so pleased, he's beaming,' Heather commented.

'Yes, Heather. It's so long since I saw that look. He's a changed man,' Pamela replied.

'I think you are wonderful, Dad.' And Heather put her arms around him and added a kiss as the champagne on ice stood ready in the bucket. Only Colin was absent, working, milking and calving cows. But Colin was now the apple of Lionel's eye.

CHAPTER THIRTY-ONE

THE WEDDING

During those last months of winter Pamela was kept busy arranging the finer points of 'The Big Day'. Lionel was happy enough to go along with his wife's and the couple's wishes.

'I don't mind waving my cheque book for this family affair, but you must get the list out and let Colin say who he wants there. His Uncle Frank should be invited, a chap I met at the pub who had guided young Colin since his father died. He's one of the old school.'

When Pamela produced the typed list of guests, Lionel's first reaction was, 'Oh, I see Colin's chosen young John Lamb, the Rector's son, as best man.'

Pamela replied, 'He's an awfully nice boy, you know. But mind you, I think Colin chose him to please me.'

'I'm glad the Williamses are coming – and of course Fiona is the chief bridesmaid. Gwyn Williams is a cut above most of the farmers round here.'

'Yes darling. Is that because he went to Cirencester Agricultural College?' Pamela knew how Lionel felt about qualifications.

Time passed and Heather's nineteenth birthday and the wedding approached. Her birthday fell on Easter Saturday that year, and Hawthorn Farm was resplendent with daffodils. The countryside had awoken from the sleep of winter for more thousands of years than could be imagined. Finally, it was here – Heather's big day, her nineteenth birthday and her wedding day.

At 6.30 that Saturday morning the villagers of Ayshon were startled when the church bells rang as dawn broke over the hills. Old George Burford had secretly got his ringers to give that early morning welcome to the special day. Pamela hadn't slept very well, worrying whether she had forgotten anything, and had just fallen asleep when the bells rang out. 'What's going on? It's half past six. What will the village think?'

Lionel, fully awake, replied, 'It's George's idea to start the day.'

'You're not getting up yet, are you dear?' Pamela asked.

'Yes. I'll get a cup of tea, then I'm going to have a look around the marquee to see if Phil has put the final touches to it.'

The wedding had been arranged for 12 o'clock. The guests from London had spent the night at a hotel in Broadway. Barbara, Jeremy and Charles were at Hawthorn Farm. Pamela's father, now Sir Claud Bennet, knighted they say because of his work for the Conservative Party, and Lady Bennet stayed at the Queens Hotel in Cheltenham.

At 11 o'clock that Saturday morning the scene at Hawthorn Farm was reminiscent of Ascot as the guests paraded on the lawn and waited for cars to transport them to the church a couple of miles away. Some of the creations worn by the ladies were the latest from London fashion houses, just out of this world. Ayshon was agog that morning. The village women in the yard of the Old Inn opposite the farm were breathless, while a few of the men stopped in their tracks as they made their way to the pub.

'Bless my soul!' one old villager said. 'What sights you see when you haven't got your gun. I'm sure that lady in the leopardskin coat is wearing two hats. Puts me in mind of a two-tier pulpit in the church.'

Lionel followed Heather around the little crowd as if he was loathe to lose her. 'We should be a few minutes late, dear, when I take you up the aisle, a sort of tradition, you know.'

Heather smiled, knowing that Lionel knew all about traditions. He fussed on. 'I want to start from here with you prompt at 12 o'clock. It's 2 miles to the church and Phil Grafton will do it comfortably in 4 minutes.'

'Okay, Daddy. I've warned Colin that we will be a few minutes late.'

At a few minutes to twelve Phil Grafton arrived at the door with the Rolls. The handsome blue car, specially polished and lacquered, looked splendid that spring morning. Phil looked anxious. The stable clock boomed out one, two, three, until on the stroke of twelve, Lionel and his daughter walked briskly through the front door of Hawthorn Farm and the few villagers who hadn't left for the church clapped and cheered. Voices called out, 'Best Wishes, Miss Heather.'

'Are you nervous, Heather?' her father questioned. 'Perhaps not as nervous as I am. Do enjoy your day.'

'Thanks, Dad. I'm glad you've taken to Colin. It makes all the difference.' She kissed him on the cheek. 'The last one I'll have', he thought, 'from an unmarried daughter.'

As Heather stepped from the car she looked stunningly beautiful. On her father's arm, they walked up the aisle as the Wedding March was played with vigour on the church organ. As millions had done before him, Colin smiled as he met his bride at the front of the church.

As the congregation sang 'Love Divine all Loves Excelling' Lionel whispered to Pamela, 'I don't care for that hymn of Wesley's, but it's a Welsh tune and will suit the Williamses no doubt.'

The well-known promises were made and the ring put on Heather's finger. After signing the Register the couple made their way down the aisle followed by the bridesmaids, smiling as the cameras clicked. Pamela shed a tear, Lionel cleared his throat. It was an emotional end to a long struggle by two young folk to realise their love, their ambition. Ayshon was a scene of some of the most picturesque splendour. At the lych gate the couple were unable to get into the Rolls where Phil was waiting: their way was barred by another surprise, this time from the Young Farmers' Club. A dozen of them had made an archway of hay forks for them to pass under, and old George Burford awaited them on the village green with Bronwyn, Heather's pony, dressed in coloured ribbons and with a sign above her bridle made by Mary Grafton: 'God bless the Bride and Groom'. Heather threw her arms around her pony and then around George Burford, giving him her bouquet of flowers. Phil then drove the couple to the reception at Hawthorn Farm.

The marquee was in the orchard among the blossoming apple trees, where once an evangelist had held meetings many years ago.

The marquee today was to celebrate the loving union between Colin and Heather. The spring flowers arranged by the villagers were a token of their love. The trestle tables laden with food stood in between aisles of colour and scent from the masses of flowers.

Here the financial wizards of London rubbed shoulders with farmers, doctors, an MP, members of the Young Farmers' Club, and family and friends. The usual speeches followed the meal, but it was Lionel Bainbridge's toast to the couple that was the most memorable. 'Ladies and Gentlemen,' he began. 'You know how specially dear our daughter Heather is to Pamela and myself. She has chosen a farmer for her husband, a chap from the group of Young Farmers. This was a great shock to me, and to say the least I was dubious about the match. Not because it was Colin she had chosen. Oh, no, but because being a Townee I had my doubts about farmers in particular. [Loud laughter from the Young Farmers] Colin has proved himself in many ways. He saved my life; but for him I would not be here today. It was touch and go when this gallant young man plucked me, as a brand from the burning, from that barbed wire fence. . . .'

At that, a voice came from the back of the marquee. It was none other than old George Burford, slightly unsteady after so much wine. His words came as a fitting end to the speeches: 'God Bless you, Sir, and your family!'

The company clapped Lionel, George, and the other speechmakers for a while before the guests left the marquee, filing across the gravel drive to Hawthorn Farm to view the presents in the drawing-room. Heather had left Colin for a while to speak to Fiona. Suddenly she came running over to her new husband, calling, 'Come quickly, darling. Look at this.'

Colin said, 'Oh, Heather, you look pale, are you all right?'

Bursting into tears, the young bride called for everyone to hear. 'Colin, it's marvellous.' She then read the card on the piano. 'To Heather and Colin. Wishing you every happiness on and off the farm. Love from Dad and Mother.'

Colin gasped. 'Oh! It's a generous cheque. This will enable us to buy another twenty cows.'

Heather threw her arms around Colin, weeping with joy on his shoulder, soaking his shirt collar with her tears. Revd Lamb, seeing Heather crying, was worried until Colin told him they were tears of joy. 'It's Dad's generosity. Just so overwhelming,' he explained.

Gwyn Williams came across to the pair and picked up the cheque. His comment was, 'I wish I had a father-in-law and a father like yours. Just think what I could do with a present like that!'

Colin and Heather ran back to the marquee where Lionel and Pamela were talking to friends. Still in tears, Heather threw her arms around her dad and Colin embraced Pamela. 'How can we thank you,' the couple said together.

'It's going to make all the difference to our dairy herd, Sir,' Colin added.

Lionel replied, 'Don't call me Sir, Colin. I'm your dad. Glad to help; expansion is the key to business, my boy.'

Later on, Lionel had a word with Gwyn and Nesta Williams in his study. He was still a newcomer to the ways of farmers. 'Now to put it bluntly, Gwyn, is there a future in Channel Island milk? All this new talk of cholesterol being bad for us, so many people seem to be having "semi-skimmed" milk today, and I see the whole countryside full of black and white Friesian cows.'

'You're right, Lionel, to a point, but the making of real cream from Channel Island milk has increased greatly, and folk are getting hooked on this "Real Ice Cream". Colin and Heather should cash in on this trade for the quality markets of Cheltenham.'

Chatting to Nesta, Pamela said, 'You know, Lionel can never get away from business.'

Nesta replied, 'Gwyn's the same. It's their life, isn't it?'

Lionel was pleased that the couple had booked a honeymoon in Jersey, although it seemed a business holiday. Pamela was a bit peeved that they hadn't been more adventurous and booked to go to the Caribbean. That evening Phil Grafton took the couple to Birmingham airport to catch a flight to Jersey.

CHAPTER THIRTY-TWO

THE HONEYMOON AND AFTER

While the couple were away on their ten-day honeymoon, measures were taken to ensure the Wren's Nest was looked after. Colin had recently engaged a student, who soon applied himself well to the round of early morning and evening milking. Mrs Gilder looked after him like a son. Uncle Frank, who had retired from farming, muscled in to give advice and help the student. In fact, Frank was proud of being in charge after some years of retirement. Lionel agreed for Phil Grafton to do any tractor work necessary.

In fact, Colin had been to Jersey before, with his parents, and remembered the tethered cows. He remembered too how the valuable grass was conserved, Jersey cabbages being part of the cows' diet too. The cabbages were still being grown and the stems still made into walking sticks. Now, many things had changed. For starters, the cows grazed small paddocks behind electric fences. (One thing that never changed, though, was that cows that left the island were never allowed to return.)

It wasn't farming all the time. Those honeymoon days were spent swimming in the warm sea, taking visits to France by hydrofoil. It was good to be away from the work and worry of farming, knowing that the Wren's Nest was in the capable hands of Uncle Frank, Phil Grafton, and the student. The anticipation of living at The Close, which the builders were busy restoring, was exciting.

The Hotel Ormoru was near the big swimming pool at St Helier. The ten days there, near the fields where Colin's own Jerseys had originated, were peaceful, and Colin talked to the farmers, always ready to learn. He even bought two walking sticks made from the cabbage stalks, one for his father-in-law and one for Pamela.

It seemed that Heather had an inkling that the builders at The Close were making a little palace under Lionel's constant supervision, but in no way would it be finished before their return. The new bathroom suite and shower and the oil-fired central heating certainly made the house more like home. On their return, Heather thought the place was gorgeous although it was only half finished.

'You can always stay with us, you know, until the builders have finished.' These words of Lionel's were kind, but Heather made up her mind that they would live at The Close.

A week later, Heather heard the news she had been longing for. She had passed her HND exams with distinction. Then, finally, the builders left the house. All Heather had to do now was decide between helping Colin on the farm and working in the house. Colin said that he could manage on the farm now he had the student.

Spring turned to summer, and what a spring it had been. The heifers all calved, just one calf was lost, a breach birth. On Midsummer's Day Pamela rang her daughter to say that Lionel had joined the Trust for Nature Conservation and that he was acting more as a consultant with his practice in Town, going only two days a week to London. George Burford by now was past active work in the garden and Phil had become more of a gardener than a chauffeur.

When Heather heard of her father's new hobby she laughed down the phone. 'Not Daddy a twitcher! It's great news.'

'Oh yes, darling. He's bought a most expensive tape recorder to record wildlife, and tomorrow morning he's coming to your spinney very early, about 4.30.'

'But we don't get up until six!'

'Just give him some breakfast at 6.30 and he will be away. It's his day to go to Town. That will give him time to change his clothes.'

Coming in from the yard, Colin asked his usual question, 'Any news from your Mum?'

'Plenty,' Heather replied. 'Dad's coming to the spinney at 4.30 tomorrow morning.'

'Pull the other one!' Colin replied.

'It's true, darling. He's going to record bird song in the spinney. The "Dawn Chorus" and all that.'

'He's not going to be a twitcher?' Colin asked.

'Not really,' Heather laughed.

Lionel arrived at The Close at precisely 6.15, dressed in a Parka jacket, green wellingtons, a deer stalker hat, and carrying his fancy new tape recorder. The young Gilders were up early that morning and breakfast was on the table ready for this up and coming countryman. When Heather saw him she smiled at Colin and said, 'Dad's arrived.'

'Yes, Dad's arrived,' Colin repeated. 'God bless him.'

CHAPTER THIRTY-THREE

MARGARET LIGHTSTONE, THE WI LEADER

As Lionel sorted out his new life, with his interest in nature conservation, and his roles as a churchwarden and a member of the Parish Council, Pamela made her own plans. The Women's Institute had been ticking over quietly, but now some of the villagers resented the influx of what they called Townees. This and the increased annual subscription had the effect of losing one or two long-standing members. But Pamela decided she would join.

The President, Margaret Lightstone, had held office for many years. She had come to the village soon after the war, having lived in South America. She was a pretty formidable body. She dressed in a cotton bushman's shirt and Bedford cord breeches, and stood about 6 feet tall. John, her husband, led a quiet life, content to sit in his study reading most mornings, then off to some old Army friend to play chess. While he led the passive life after his Army career, just seeing a few folk at the Old Inn, or at a British Legion meeting, Margaret was often seen around the village. In private, it seemed that Margaret and John lived in splendid isolation, John having the back part of the house with the bedroom above, and Margaret the front. It seemed a reasonable way for two free spirits to exist!

Margaret was a hard worker, despite her age, and had plans for her garden. So, up came the fence, which divided the bridle path from the garden, and Margaret planted rows and rows of raspberries, cultivated blackberries, loganberries. But that fence by the bridle path had enabled Tom Harding to drive his cattle to his field beyond without them straying. Tom and Old Bill, his stockman, had only one right of way to the Langit field, and that was along that bridle path. The first time Tom turned out his bullocks from the yard he and Bill tried, without success, to keep them to the bridle way, but without a fence it was impossible! They romped, they charged around the alleys of cordoned fruit. Some damage was done, inevitably, and Margaret phoned Tom Harding, using language quite alien to the WI, or the Mothers' Union, of which she was also a member. Margaret habitually called the working folk of Ayshon by their surname, but the names she gave to Tom Harding and Bill were somewhat different.

Margaret grew her crops, and bought vegetables from the villagers to sell on her WI stall in Evesholme. Apart from his farming, Tom Harding, whom she of course called 'Harding', grew some market garden crops, sprouts in particular, and supplied them for Margaret's stall.

'I don't want any more of your sprouts, Harding,' she announced to him in the lane. 'I'm having some very good ones cheaper from Lampit.'

Tom smiled, telling her that Lampit did not have any sprouts on his allotment, but was picking them from a farmer's field over the hedge. Lampit was what is known as light-fingered and the farmer's sprouts were said to have the 'The Finger Blight'.

Margaret also sold goat's milk and cheese at her stall, and was often seen hanging on to a chained Nanny goat on her way to a Billy at Ramacre. Some of the tales about Margaret Lightstone are hard to believe, but it is said she once took the Nanny to a neighbouring farm to mate it with a Jersey bull!

Margaret was a regular collector for charities and for Poppy Day. At a thatched cottage in a row some called Bachelors Avenue a young couple from Yorkshire, with a baby boy, had settled in. A knock at the door brought the young mother to the door with her baby on her arm sucking a dummy.

'Take that filthy thing out of that child's mouth!' This demand from Margaret raised the blood pressure of the ex-land girl. Just imagine what the reply was! The bit of broad Yorkshire logic took the WI President by surprise, it is certain. Oh, the lass bought a couple of poppies, but they say that Margaret Lightstone had her come-uppance.

But Margaret had done a good job at the WI. She was forward-looking and after one meeting Pamela came home amazed. She was in stitches as she recited to Lionel, 'Mrs Lightstone is having someone to speak on the contraceptive pill next meeting. "All in favour?" she asked the members. "It is very topical, we all see the unwanted pregnancies. All in favour?" "No," said Mrs Brown, who keeps the Post Office. Mrs Brown is seventy-five, you know.'

Lionel, reading the parish magazine, puffed his pipe and replied, 'Better to be safe than sorry.'

'Really Lionel, you are the limit!'

Margaret Lightstone then announced, at a meeting before Christmas, that the carol singing in the village would start at the garage and finish at the Old Inn.

'Why that way round?' one member said. 'Last year we started at the Old Inn and finished at the garage.'

'That's just the reason,' came the quick answer.

Despite her strange ways, Margaret Lightstone did a good job leading the WI.

CHAPTER THIRTY-FOUR

THE OLD AND THE NEW FOLK

At a neighbouring village a couple of miles from Ayshon a very substantial Georgian manor house had been on the market for some time. The Elms was an imposing residence, with a small garden in front fenced by some fine iron railings, and a fruit orchard behind the back yard. The varieties grown in the acre of gnarled trees were known only by some of the old folk of the villages – apples such as Drunken Willies, Crumps Kernals, Sourings, a whole mixture of yellow branches laden with mistletoe and covered with moss.

Old Walter, the bachelor recluse who owned The Elms, had recently died. His younger days had been spent hunting the fox, and sometimes hunting ladies, widows and spinsters. Walter was game but as time went on he had changed his image from the suave Casanova, pink tunic, classy breeches and black bowler, to the Walter we knew in greasy moleskin trousers and an old corduroy jacket.

Walter had gone to ground in a way at The Elms and the house aged with him. Although the house was cold, Walter survived, living by his frying pan and his cider – 'Keeps away the 'flu germs, that cider,' Walter claimed. Flitches of yellow bacon hung from the walls in his big kitchen, from the pigs he kept in the orchard. Every night by the glow of his oil lamp, Walter simmered a saucepan of cider, flavoured with rosemary, over the red embers of his open fire, and a jacket potato sat side by side with the saucepan. The cider and the potato smeared with butter was supper for Walter.

Walter deserved his peaceful death in hospital. He had befriended many in his past years and was an honest horse coper, a rarity. A fine rider to hounds, he treated his numerous ladies with an old-fashioned respect. Some said 'poor old Walter' but his life had been the life of a man who did what pleased him.

The estate agent's notice board had become yellow with age. No one had fallen for The Elms. The outside was appealing, the iron railings were a feature, as was the old oak front door. But inside, the dampness, mould, and neglect gave a chill feeling. It was a somewhat spooky place. The old wallpaper peeled from the walls and the staircase was worm-eaten.

A gentleman from Birmingham, Arthur Monkton, owned some pasture land a few miles away from The Elms. He kept a few race horses, looked after by a groom in a cottage in the fields. Arthur was a turf accountant in town but he and his wife, Pat, had recently had a win on the football pools. Recently? Well, that was ten years ago! He invested in The Elms, turned the house into a home, and Pat took over as President of Ayshon WI when Margaret Lightstone stepped down.

Although Pat Monkton was a successful President, she was viewed with suspicion by the local families. Old Mrs Brown at the Post Office said, 'The Monktons may be high fliers but there's something dubious about them. They may be well off and kind but they are not quality.' George Burford put it more bluntly when he said, 'They be jumped up.'

Pat Monkton was what George called 'a boiling piece'. She had a Diana Dors figure and she knew it. Her conversation with Pamela Bainbridge at the monthly meeting always turned to Ascot and fashions, and she spoke of the 'London Season'. Pamela tried to guide her to the more practical matters of village life.

Walter's old house was transformed by the Monktons into a very attractive part of the village. Garden parties for the church were held in the summer, under the trees in the old orchard where the grass was manicured like the green of a golf course. The WI held their meetings in the summer in the walled-in garden at the side of the house. Pamela and Pat became friends, but not close friends, it has to be said.

Lionel Bainbridge sometimes had an evening with Arthur, and introduced him as a member to his Cheltenham Club. They had one thing in common: Lionel had spent a lifetime working in finance, and what Arthur didn't know about making money didn't matter. The money he had won on the football pools was well invested. Arthur knew how many beans made five.

Arthur drove a new Porsche, which he parked outside the wrought iron railings of The Elms next to the Post Office. One morning, a Thursday, when the pensioners of the village were at the Post Office drawing what George Burford called 'their Lloyd George', Arthur was leaning against his new car as the sun shone on the gleaming blue paint work and the silver-like chrome. He was holding his mobile telephone and talking quite loudly to someone in Birmingham. George Burford, who had never seen a mobile phone before, stood watching in awe outside the Post Office, then nipped back inside to tell Mrs Brown, who had given him his pension.

'Anything wrong, George? I hope your pension's okay.'

'Yes, Mrs Brown,' came the reply. 'But Master Monkton's outside here with a piece of black plastic in his hand talking to somebody.'

'That's his mobile phone, George; they are all the rage today.'

George thought a while, then replied, 'Perhaps he's talking to God – he's talking very loud.'

Above the fields at the back of Hawthorn Farm, under the wood, a small enclosure grew wild daffodils. At the weekend, when the flowers were at their best, Pamela opened the field gate and put up a sign that read: FOR 20p HELP YOURSELF TO DAFFODILS. IN AID OF THE NURSING ASSOCIATION. Folks came from far and near, gipsies in particular. They picked masses of blooms, paid George Burford at the field gate, then sold the bunches in The Promenade in Cheltenham.

Meanwhile, Pat was concerned about the cider drinkers in the villages. Men were drinking to excess at a neighbouring pub. Fights were commonplace. Wives were being assaulted by their menfolk, drinking too much of what was commonly known as 'Agricultural

Brandy'. It was fighting cider all right, and one man quite addicted to it was Percy Comberton.

Percy and his wife, Bertha, lived in a cottage high on the hill. One Saturday night he came home a bit the worse for wear to find that Bertha had locked him out. The front door had a glass panel, which enabled him to break in. Sunday morning was spent by this farm-worker removing the glass from a picture frame to mend the glass in the door.

Bertha, a loyal member of the WI, had not attended for a while and Pat was concerned, knowing about her husband's intemperate habits. Bertha had produced six children and Percy was unconcerned whether they added to the number or not. Bertha and her sister moved a bed downstairs for him. She remained in the bedroom, and lived downstairs in the daytime in the kitchen by the range. It was a hard life for her with a man so inconsiderate.

Concerned about the Combertons, Pat sent a parcel of groceries to the cottage on the hill. She said at a WI committee meeting, 'You know, I don't like the way that family lingers rather than lives up on the Hill. You are on the Council, could you recommend them for a council house?'

Margaret Lightstone smiled, saying, 'I'll try, but who's going to pay the rent? You know Percy is a bad payer.'

Percy had made it known that he had ferrets for sale. The surprise was where he kept those ferrets – in the front room, which was his bedroom too. The bed was in front of a log fire. Percy had a 4-gallon barrel of cider, with a tap fixed, on a shelf by the fireside. From here he could draw a mug of cider from his bed during the night. His bar was open all hours. When the fire was not lit, the ferrets would play on the hearth, taking turns to climb the chimney. Percy would sit smoking a drooping Woodbine cigarette and wearing boxing gloves. (He had fancied himself in the ring many years back when some cauliflower-eared professional was taking on all-comers at Evesholme Mop Fair.)

'Take your pick if you want a ferret,' he would say. 'Pick up the one you fancy.' Most of the prospective buyers declined this offer.

Those ferrets looked pretty nippy. On the hearth the young ones and the old fitcher lapped up bread and milk from a saucer. When the time came, Percy would entice the ferrets back into their box at the fireside – wearing his boxing gloves.

Over on the other side of the room stood a very handsome piano, gleaming white like ivory. Percy told the story of how he 'got it on the Never Never'.

Percy's tale was quite a sad one. Before the cider got hold of him, like an ever-tightening noose, he could have been goalkeeper for the village football team, he was athletic and strong.

Round the corner of the cottage, Percy kept other animals too. By a Jargonelle pear tree, now leafless, a kennel with a chain attached gave the impression that this man had a dog. But no! The kennel was home to a very sly-looking young fox. It would come to Percy, who stroked it lovingly, but it bared its teeth if strangers were present. Sometimes Percy would take him for a walk to the pub, but as Percy himself said, 'I don't stay long these days. No need to with cider on tap.'

Another tea chest under the pear tree housed a couple of jackdaws and Percy exchanged words with them. Back in the house, he played a few well-known pieces on his piano, and Bertha brought the tea to the table. Four of their children were away working in the Midlands, the two youngest were asleep in the spare bedroom.

Percy and Bertha got their council house, but Percy never settled in a modern property without the fox, the jackdaws, his ferrets, and the 4-gallon barrel by the fireside, so Bertha had a respite as her husband drifted back to the inn. His piano went back to the hire purchase company, as it was on the 'Never Never'.

CHAPTER THIRTY-FIVE

COLIN AND HEATHER
AT THE CLOSE

The farm at the Wren's Nest in Ramacre hamlet now had the new Jersey heifers among the herd. The milk was taken by tanker to the local 'Real Ice-Cream' factory, where the demand for this special brand snowballed. With the increase in the herd, Colin was able to employ a full-time worker, Phil and Mary Grafton's son, David, a useful chap of eighteen. He was handy with the tractor, silage cutting and baling during the long days of summer.

Colin didn't want his young wife to be for ever working in the dairy, lugging bales of hay and sacks of cattle cake. Mrs Gilder, too, was worried that Heather would over-do things, but it suited her during the early months of her marriage. The girl seemed to delight in being a farmer's wife, so different from the old image. In her Indian cotton shirt and jeans, Heather was the apple of Colin's eye. He had won her, despite so much opposition from Lionel. It was all well worth it.

The Close was now furnished in keeping with its eighteenth-century style. Lionel delighted in furniture sales, he loved a bargain. He took his daughter to house furniture sales all over the Cotswolds and in the Vale.

Lionel and Pamela often visited The Close. Pamela enjoyed telling her daughter tales about the WI, and was disappointed that she didn't want to join. But Heather had her reasons. 'It's early days in our marriage, Mother. Colin likes me at home in the evenings, and somehow I don't think I'd fit in with the well-meaning do-gooders at the Institute.' However, the tales were entertainment indeed.

Sometimes Barbara and Jeremy, and Heather's brother, Charles, spent weekends with them too, glad to be away from London for a while. Lionel enjoyed these family times, and looked forward to grandchildren at The Close. 'Now the place is furnished,' he said to Pamela, 'and young David Grafton works for them, children for them, grandchildren for us, would be wonderful.'

He was pretty observant, and one evening he had an idea that his daughter was what George Burford would describe as 'in the family way'. But he kept his thoughts to himself until he and Pamela were on their way home. He started to laugh softly, a contented laugh. 'What on earth's the matter, darling?' Pamela asked.

'Nothing is the matter, Pamela. I've noticed something.'

'What is it, Lionel. Tell me, I insist.'

'You're going to be a grandmother. Heather's expecting.'

'Are you sure, Lionel? She's said nothing to me. You are joking.'

'No. You'll find I'm right. It's great news.'

The next morning Pamela was at The Close soon after breakfast. Colin and Heather were having coffee after the morning's milking. 'What's wrong, Mother, being here so early?' they wondered.

Pamela, now rather flushed, replied, 'I couldn't sleep last night after what Daddy said. He said you're expecting a baby.'

'Perfectly true, Mummy. I was going to call you on Sunday. The baby is due in April.'

Pamela threw her arms around her daughter, then around Colin, saying, 'I'm so happy for you both.' A party was arranged that autumn when family and friends celebrated the news, and so the story of Hawthorn Farm looked set to continue.